LOSING
Normal

THREE WOMEN · THREE STORIES OF HOPE

For Tracy,
I sure hope
our travels bring
us together again! I
Loved the time we
spent together!
Fondly,
Sally Spencer
06·23·2023

HEATHER CHENEY · SALLY SPENCER · PATTIE ZYLKA

Losing Normal

Three Women • Three Stories of Hope

By Heather Cheney, Sally Spencer and Pattie Zylka

© 2007 Heather Cheney, Sally Spencer and Pattie Zylka

ISBN: 0974696722

(978-0-9746967-2-0)

Library of Congress Control Number: 2007933513

Published by LegacyONE, Kirkland, WA

Cover Photos by danielgarciaphotography.com, San Jose, CA

Graphic Design by Louise Holder, Holder's Ink, Kirkland, WA

Printed by Gorham Printing, Centralia, WA

Printed in the United States of America

All Scripture quotations from *The Holy Bible, New International Version*

© 1978- by New York International Bible Society

FROM THE THREE OF US

to God

FOR HIS PROMISE OF HOPE
AND A FUTURE.

Foreword

A ROCK, A LITTLE MAN, AND THREE WOMEN

Sally Shares...

One warm summer evening, in July of 1996, I was attending a Team in Training information meeting. I committed that evening to run a marathon and to raise money for the Leukemia/Lymphoma Society. One month into my marathon training, I was widowed. Suddenly, unexpectedly, out of nowhere, my life changed in a heartbeat. I lost normal .

I knew that I would be unable to grieve, help my children deal with our loss, work, AND train for a marathon. So I made the decision to donate the money I had raised to a Team in Training teammate that I had become close to. As Melissa prepared to run the marathon I told her that my heart and my energy would be with her every step of the way and if she ever felt that she could not run another step, she should picture my hands gently on her back pushing her forward.

On a crisp winter day, in early December 1996, Melissa completed her first marathon. When she came to share her experience with me she brought with her an interesting gift. It was a six-inch wire sculpture of a man with outstretched arms and flexed hands. And there was a granite rock the size of a baseball. Melissa placed the little mans flexed hands against the granite rock and she explained that during the marathon when she did not know if she could run another step, she pictured my hands on her back gently pushing her forward, giving her the strength to go on. She wanted me to know that when my grief became unbearable and I didn't know how I would go on, that I should picture all the people who loved me with their hands gently on my back helping me to push my boulder of grief up the mountain to healing.

That little man pushing the boulder became a symbol of hope for me. Every time I looked at it I felt love, and hope, and God's grace.

One day, many months later, I looked at the little man and the boulder and I flipped him over the boulder like he was doing a handstand. I stepped back, tilted my head, and smiled. The boulder didn't seem so huge or heavy anymore. It was more of a rock and I was doing a handstand on top of it, not pushing it. I was healing...

For almost six years I kept the rock and the little man in a special place where I could look at it many times during the day. I thought that I would always keep it close to me, as a reminder of hope. It was my special symbol. That all changed when my very dear friend, Pattie, was diagnosed with breast cancer. All of a sudden, out of nowhere, her life changed. I knew immediately that the best gifts I could give Pattie were love and hope.

So I went shopping for some very specific items. I bought her some sleepwear for her hospital stay (feminine enough for her to know that she would still be sexy), a cozy flannel nightgown with an oreo cookie and milk pattern on it (for days she just wanted to curl up), and I bundled up my little man and my rock to pass on to her. I would shower her with my love, and I would give her my hope.

I wrapped everything, and headed off to visit Pattie at work. I walked into her office, hugged her hard, then sat down and started handing her the gifts I had brought for her. First, I gave her the sleepwear, then the cozy flannel nightgown. Finally, I shared my story of hope as I pulled my rock and my little man out of their bag and offered them to her. As she took them in her hands I told her to keep them as long as she wanted or needed, and when she was ready, to pass the rock and the little man on to another woman who needed hope. And when she passed them on, to tell my story and her story to the woman who received them.

As I left Pattie's office that day, my heart was remembering when I had lost normal. I did not want that for my friend. I could not heal Pattie...but I had passed on my hope.

Pattie Shares...

Weary. That's how I felt as I sat at my desk at work that day. I was one week away from the date that was circled on my calendar, July 29, 2002. In the two-inch square, underneath that date, was the dreaded word mastectomy. Concentrating was nearly impossible. I found myself mindlessly pushing papers around my desk, moving them from one pile to the next, waiting for the clock to release me for the day. My paper shuffling was brought to a halt by the cheerful voice of my friend Sally. Arms loaded with gifts, she came bounding into my office. Along with some fun gifts to lift my spirits, she had a special gift carefully wrapped in tissue paper. She tenderly unwrapped the treasure that was nestled inside. A rock and a little wire man came tumbling out from the white tissue, and as it did, Sally explained to me that I now had this big "boulder" of grief called breast cancer, that I had to push up the mountain of healing. She went on to say, that if there came a time when I thought I couldn't continue on, I was to picture all the people I love with their hands on my back helping me push this rock.

The gift came with one string attached. When I had worked through my grief and loss, I was to pass the man and rock along to another woman going through crises.

The rock and the man sat on my desk for almost a year. At times I had him surfing on top of the rock... not quite doing a handstand but getting close. The day finally did come, when I realized I had worked through my sadness and the little man changed position. He flipped over from pushing the rock to a celebrating handstand! I couldn't help but think, who would be the next woman to receive this symbol of hope.

In June of 2003 I knew exactly who the recipient would be. I carefully wrapped up the rock and little man and got in my car and drove to Heather's house. As I was ringing the doorbell I was so aware that this rock and little man now had two stories attached to it, and Heather would soon be adding her own story of loss, grief and hope.

Heather Shares…

Sad. Depressed. Scared. Numb. These are all the things that I was feeling the night that Pattie rang my doorbell. I was in my favorite pajamas, and watching TV, trying to leave reality for a few minutes, and forget that my life had drastically changed. I was three months pregnant and had just found out that my baby had less than a one percent chance of survival. Having a normal pregnancy was no longer a possibility for me.

It was at this point that Pattie gave me the man and the rock, and explained the significance, and that it had originally come from Sally. As she spoke I felt like I was being welcomed into this special club: a club of people that God had brought through something extraordinary. I had mixed feelings about this; on the one hand I looked at Pattie and thought, "she's been through a horrible year, but at least she has a stronger relationship with God and her husband." I remember thinking that maybe it was my turn for God to do something amazing with my life. Then I cringed, as my heart screamed, "No, wait. God I can't do this. I didn't want to sign up for something this hard." I felt like if I accepted the man and the rock it would mean I was accepting the fact that my baby would die. In my heart I still held onto the belief that God might heal her, and I did not think that this was something that I would need.

As Pattie spoke she explained how symbolic the man and the rock had been for her, and reminded me that God would see me through to the other side of this difficult time in my life.

I have had the man and the rock for almost three years now and while I continue to struggle with grief and loss, I believe that the man and the rock have served their purpose, and I am praying for the next person who will receive them.

At the time of publication (summer 2007) the rock and the little man statue have moved to Italy. I passed it on to a friend of mine and Adams' who had a miscarriage.

Contents

SALLY'S STORY

ONE: The Widow's Club...15
TWO: Is There Someone There With You?...17
THREE: When Life Went Gray...19
FOUR: God, I Do Not Want to Do This...23
FIVE: A Graceful Boulder...25
SIX: Where Are All the Hurting People?...27
SEVEN: That "W" Word...29
EIGHT: Hunting for Survival...31
NINE: Who's In My Closet?...35
TEN: 365 Days...39
ELEVEN: My Two Sons...41
TWELVE: Lifelines: Grab on, Hold Tight...45
THIRTEEN: Aftershocks and the Global Worrier...49
FOURTEEN: Don't Sweat the Small Stuff...53
EPILOGUE: April 2007...57

PATTIE'S STORY

ONE: Breast Cancer and Kitchen Ants...65
TWO: Admission Into Club Loss...69
THREE: Where Are All the Hurting People?...73

FOUR: I Don't Want to Do This Anymore!...75

FIVE: Darkness of Despair...77

SIX: Enough Light for the Next Step...81

SEVEN: I Want My Old Life Back, But—...85

EIGHT: Surviving vs. Thriving...89

NINE: Cold Nipples and Winding Roads...95

TEN: The View From My Rear View Mirror...99

ELEVEN: Swedish Aftershocks...103

TWELVE: Where Are My Ants?...105

EPILOGUE: April 2007...107

HEATHER'S STORY

ONE: Oh Baby, My Baby...115

TWO: Then Our Doctor Dropped the Bomb...119

THREE: A Mother's Love...123

FOUR: God, I'll Make You a Deal...127

FIVE: Trust and Surrender...129

SIX: I Want *My* Mommy...133

SEVEN: The Hardest Days...137

EIGHT: Surviving Thanksgiving...139

NINE: What Is This Thing Called Closure?...143

TEN: Little Earthquakes...147

ELEVEN: Mother's Day and EPT...149

TWELVE: Cloud 9 of Hope...151

THIRTEEN: Brown Grass, Green Grass...153

EPILOGUE: April 2007...157

Sally's STORY

To my sons . . .

ADAM,
who taught me strength,
and

KEVIN,
who taught me acceptance.
I love you.

CHAPTER

One

THE WIDOW'S CLUB

*I*f I were to give you just one clue about myself, it would be that I really do not have control issues. I just like to think of myself as highly organized. You probably know what I'm talking about. The kind of organized that when you get ready to go on a trip, you line up the bags by the front door in the order in which they should be loaded into the car. And I'm not sure why this is, but no one else seems to be able to make everything fit into the Suburban just right.

Now sometimes highly organized people expect themselves to be able to do it all, handle anything, no problem. But ah, there is a problem with that line of thinking because it encourages a false sense of control. Until that one day, that one day when this huge boulder of heartache falls out of nowhere, right in front of you, blocking your path.

You can't go around it. You can't go through it. You just have to push that boulder up the steepest hill you have ever seen. So you place your hands on the boulder, you dig your feet in, and you try to inch it up the hill. You make a little progress. You think to yourself, "I've got it. I can do it." And then you suddenly lose your footing. Before you know it, you're lying flat on your back with the darn thing on your stomach. Now what?

So you slowly, slowly wiggle yourself out from under the boulder, stand with your hands on your hips and mutter under your breath, "I will do this." This time, you decide to put your back against the boulder, use your legs, and push it up the hill that way. After all, everyone knows that is how you move something heavy. Slowly, ever so slowly, up the hill you go. You are elated because you are doing it. You're doing it!

Then...*whoa!* Wait! What's happening? Well, you guessed it. The boulder rolls back down. It rolls back down rather forcibly, folding you in half, and it is now resting comfortably once again, this time on your back. And you are stuck, stuck folded over with your ears between your knees.

It takes a lot for some of us to realize that we are not really the ones in control. For me it took the sudden, unexpected death of my husband. Loss. Huge, horrible, unexpected, unwanted, go-away-and-leave-me-alone loss.

If someone had asked me if I wanted to join the widow's club, I would have sat on my hands, lowered my head, kept my eyes downcast, and prayed they wouldn't pick me. But there I was, forced into a club that no one wants to belong to, and there was no way out.

CHAPTER

Two

IS THERE SOMEONE THERE WITH YOU?

I have visited this day, the day my husband died, time and again. I have looked at it every way that I know how. And, I have come to realize that God began preparing me many years ago.

The small California town in which I grew up had only two cemeteries. My grandmother lived just a few blocks from one of the cemeteries. When I was about six years old, my uncle and I would walk to the cemetery to visit relatives buried there. I loved the family stories Uncle Pete told me as we walked and paid our respects. I was intrigued by his stories and also by how comfortable he was there. Little did I know that feeling of being comfortable at a cemetery was to become a precious gift.

I am the oldest of three girls. One evening, when I was babysitting my younger sisters, the phone rang. A deep male voice asked first for my father and then for my mother. When I explained that they were not available, he identified himself as a sheriff and asked how old I was. I told him I was sixteen. He then asked, *"Is there someone there with you?"*

"Yes," I replied, "I am babysitting my younger sisters." He went on to say he was sorry for having to let me know in this way, but my Great Aunt Caroline had died. I took down the information for my parents and thanked him for calling. I have never forgotten his compassionate question, *"Is there someone there with you?"*

In the fourteen months before my husband died, I attended four funerals. Each one caused me to pause and reflect. Three of the deaths were anticipated because of illnesses; one death was brutally sudden. All four deaths left grieving family members that coped differently with their loss. I learned something from each of these deaths.

But the brutally sudden death of a family acquaintance, a mother with two teen-aged children, had enormous impact on me. She was a Christian, and her husband and children had a great love for God. They were comforted by their knowledge and belief that she was with God. I was amazed. I remember thinking that my children did not have that kind of a foundation. If something were to happen to me, how would they go on without those kinds of beliefs?

Oh, I believed in God, and I had attended church over the years. I was always grateful and aware of the blessings that He had given me. Still, I visited Him sporadically. So, when Carol died, I made a decision to go on what I called "a church search." I would find a church where I, and my youngest son, could grow and learn, and feel welcome and comfortable. We found our church just six weeks before my husband died. I am so grateful that we did.

CHAPTER

Three

WHEN LIFE WENT GRAY

On Tuesday, August 27, 1996, it is 4:30 in the morning when I hear the noises associated with my husband preparing to go hunting. It is to be the first hunt of the season for him, and he is going with my father and a friend, Tim. He is so excited about a day with the boys, he's like a little kid. Trying to be quiet only makes everything he does seem louder. I am asleep, but in that twilight where you are aware, but still asleep. I hear Sandro rummaging through one of his drawers. When I ask him what he is looking for he says he cannot find his special binoculars. I almost laugh because he has four or five pairs of "special binoculars." Instead, I drift back into my twilight sleep.

I am aware that he is sitting on the bed next to me watching me sleep. He strokes my arm gently and leans over to kiss me good-bye. I snuggle deeper into the covers knowing that I have about 30 more minutes of sleep before my alarm will signal the start of my day.

About 8 a.m. my husband calls me while they are on the road to Paso Robles. I am really glad to hear from him because I had not said, "Good-bye. Have a great time. Be safe and good luck!" We speak briefly and hang up the phone cheerfully. I almost call him back because he didn't say "I love you" before we hung up. Instead, I remember that he's with the boys and I smile. As I finish getting ready for work I am thinking about the dirty hunting clothes that will need washing when he gets home that night.

I am at work that day, creating a design for a company shirt, when the announcement that my father is on Line 2 comes over the intercom.

I pick up the phone and it is dead. No one is there. I walk out of my office to let customer service know that there was no one on the line. As I am doing so, they tell me my father has called back and is again on Line 2. With the new shirt logo and a red pen in hand, I answer the phone.

I notice immediately that my father is really choked up. With tears in his voice, he tells me that my husband has had what appears to be a heart attack, and that he has been airlifted to a nearby hospital. I hear the weighted seriousness in his voice. I hear the pain, the choking emotion, and still I ask, "You're kidding, aren't you?"

"No," he tells me. Then, with his voice like I have never heard it before, he says, "And honey, it doesn't look good."

As my father and Tim drive to the hospital, I hurriedly get the name of the hospital from them so that I can call on Sandro's status. Then I tell my father to please, please, please drive safely because I would not be able to bear it if something happened to them. He assures me they will, but I picture them barreling down the road, as fast as they can, to be with my husband, a man they also loved.

I quickly call home and speak to my oldest son, Adam. It is his second day of college, and he is home from school and watching his brother Kevin, who is six years younger. They are playing checkers. I tell my son: "Grandpa just called and it looks like Dad may have had a heart attack. Don't say anything to your brother, but, driving *very* slowly, please come to the office." We live only a few minutes from my workplace yet I say to him: "Drive slowly please, because I couldn't bear it if something happened to the two of you." It is the second time in five minutes that I have spoken those words to people I love.

With stunned co-workers gathered around me, I call information to get the phone number of the hospital where my husband has been taken. I dial the number and explain to the woman who answers that my husband has been airlifted to the hospital. She immediately connects me to the emergency room. A woman answers the phone. I give her my name, and again explain that my husband has just been airlifted to the hospital. She asks me if he is the one who had been hunting. I tell her that he is. She asks me to hold, and tells me that she will get the doctor for me right away.

I am relieved and hopeful. If she is getting the doctor, my husband must be okay. While I am waiting for the doctor to come to the phone my mind is racing. *How am I going to get to the hospital as quickly as possible?* It's nearly five hours away!

Suddenly, a deep male voice says my name. He identifies himself as my husband's doctor, and then he asks, *"Is there someone there with you?"*

At that moment, I knew exactly what he was going to say to me because I had been asked that very question 27 years before. Over the phone, in the afternoon, while I was at work, came the news. My husband was dead.

I shake my head no, to let my co-workers know he did not make it. Then, as I turn around, I realize that my sons have walked in, and they have seen me shake my head…no.

CHAPTER

Four

GOD, I DO NOT WANT TO DO THIS

I really am a detail-oriented person, but I do not want to attend to these necessary details. I am planning my husband's funeral. No, not now. Not yet. He is only 52. He is way too young. How can I be talking to coroners, mortuaries, and cemeteries? I should be talking about washing my husband's dirty hunting clothes, not making arrangements to bring his body back home. This should not be happening. Why is this happening? Oh, God, I do not want to do this. But oh, if I have to do this, would you please help me?

Twenty-four hours after my husband died, I stop by work briefly. I have to sign a letter that needs to go out to our clients and I want to pick up some pictures of my husband that I keep in my office. I need the pictures for the memory board my sisters and I are putting together for his memorial service. When I walk into the office, one of our customer service reps looks at me and says, "You look awful." What is she thinking? Is she thinking? Is she expecting me to be myself, to put a smile on my face and pretend that everything is okay? Does she want me to be okay so she will feel better? I look at her, stunned by her words, and walk quietly past.

Sandro died Tuesday afternoon and came home on Wednesday evening. I visit him at the mortuary that night. Everyone is worried about me doing this, but I know I need to do it. I have to see him. I have to tell him I love him one more time. I have to say good-bye.

My father and my youngest sister, Sandy, drive with me to the mortuary. I leave them in the waiting room and go with the kind young man who tells me he will be staying with my husband tonight. He takes me down the hall, around the corner and just before we enter the room, he softly says to me, "Don't look under the blanket." At my request, there has been an autopsy; he is trying to protect me. I enter the room and there is my husband. He looks so peaceful, as if he is sleeping. His head is resting on a pillow, and there is a brown and white plaid blanket tucked around him. I place my hand on his head and gently smooth his hair. I trace the outline of his face, his nose, his lips, and I lay my head on his chest as I begin to say my good-bye. When I am done, I walk back to the waiting room to join my father and my sister. As I enter the room, they stop talking, stand up, and immediately come toward me. I quietly tell them that I am better for having seen him.

It is now Thursday. I have lost 12 pounds in two days. Today is the first day of seventh grade for my 12-year-old son (ouch) and it is Visitation Day at the mortuary.

They give you things at the mortuary. I didn't really know that before. I have always associated small, velvet drawstring pouches with something wonderful. In the movies, on television, and in real life, they usually hold an exciting surprise or a beautiful treasure. I am given such a pouch at the mortuary, in the late afternoon, just as the sun is going down, on the day of the visitation service. When I look in the pouch, I swallow hard and hold it tight. Inside are my husband's watch and wedding ring.

His wedding ring should be on his finger. It was always on his finger. He never took it off. But here it is, in a small, velvet drawstring pouch, never to be worn by him again.

When I get home that night I put his wedding ring on a gold chain and clasp the chain around my neck. The chain is fairly long and makes the ring fall close to my heart. Close to my heart, never far, always close, but he is never going to hold me again.

Finally, the day is over. I have completed Visitation Day. They call it Visitation Day, but it is actually the last time I will ever look at my husband. Why do they call it Visitation Day?

CHAPTER

Five

A GRACEFUL BOULDER

It is barely after midnight and a brand new day has begun. It is Friday, three days since my husband died. And today is the day that we will bury him, the day that we will hold his memorial service.

Since Sandro died, I feel in my heart that God has been with me. There is no other way that I can explain it. There is no other way that I would be able to handle this huge boulder called grief. There is no other way I would know just what to do. It is as if He has downloaded the information into my very being. He has placed compassionate people around me, and He has given me the grace to deal with the challenges. I am grateful. But today...how do I face today?

As I walk into my bedroom, I think about what this day will hold. I close my bedroom door and stretch out my arms and say to God, "I cannot do this on my own. Here I am. Please, help me." Then I drop to my knees, and I ask God to surround me with His love, and to help me feel love, truth, honesty, and light. And oh...how He does.

I wake in the early morning, and prepare myself for the day. I am calm and peaceful, with a clear sense of purpose. I am honoring my husband today. I am celebrating his life with the people that loved and cared for him. I will do this well. I will make Sandro proud.

I have chosen to have a private burial first, then to celebrate his life with a memorial service. For us, I believe, this is the right choice. The burial is strangely peaceful. I feel my husband there; I feel God close beside me, and I feel the love of both. And when the burial is over, we quietly leave the cemetery for the memorial service.

When we arrive at the memorial service, I am reminded again that my prayers have been answered. I feel love and truth, honesty and light, and I know God is protecting me and holding me tight. I remember the verse that I have been repeating to myself over and over again. Jeremiah 29:11, *"For I know the plans I have for you,"* declares the Lord, *"plans to prosper you and not to harm you, plans to give you hope and a future."*

With my sons sitting on either side of me, the memorial service begins. I listen closely to every word. I rest my hands on theirs and I thank God for them. When it is my turn to speak, I calmly walk to the podium to share what I believe God has placed in my heart. And I share that it doesn't matter how much time we have with someone we love. We always yearn for that one more moment...just that one more moment.

CHAPTER

Six

WHERE ARE ALL THE HURTING PEOPLE?

I sleep on my husband's side of the bed now, and I do not want to wash his pillowcase because I want to remember his smell. In the evening, I wear his sweatshirts because that is the closest I can get to his arms wrapped around me. One day I go into his office and listen to his voicemail greeting over and over and over again because I want to hear the sound of his voice.

I need to be close to him. I need to stay close to him. I need him back.

What is wrong with everyone? I feel like my skin has been peeled off of my body and that I am a raw, oozing mess. Why is everyone looking at me like I am normal? Can't they see how raw I am?

Everywhere I look there are people going about their normal days. They are grocery shopping, dropping off kids at school, and getting frustrated with normal, hectic, daily schedules. They are naïve; they do not realize life can change in a heartbeat. Normal? There is no normal for me right now, but I remember normal. Oh, how I want normal back.

It is one week since we buried my husband, and I take my youngest son downtown to get some frozen yogurt. It has always been a treat for us to do this together, and I hope it will be good for both of us. The man who usually serves us yogurt asks how everything is going. He has a smile on his face as he helps us, and he looks up to hear my response.

I want to be able to tell him that everything is great, to smile and ask about his day. But I cannot do this. We have been coming to his shop for years, and he will find out eventually, so I tell him my husband has just died. His eyes show immediate compassion. He has kind words for us. We know that he is sorry for our loss. Our loss. There it is again. Our loss, never to be found. No more normal.

We decide to walk through town as we eat our frozen yogurt. Moving seems to help. As we turn the corner, we run into my son's first soccer coach. "Hey," he says. "How's it going? What's new?"

What's new? How do I answer that one? Can't he see that I have no skin on my body, that I am raw, that my son is clearly hurting? I tell him quietly that my husband died last week. His eyes widen. He shakes his head and says he is so sorry. He ruffles my son's hair and he moves on, away from our nightmare.

Where are all the hurting people? Where are the people that could take one look at us and know that we have suffered a huge, huge loss? Frozen yogurt may not have been a good idea after all.

CHAPTER

Seven

THAT "W" WORD

I have been a widow for eight days. I am only 43. I am too young to be a widow. How I hate that word, that *"W"* word. Who thought of that word in the first place? What an absolutely stupid word! I am not going to use that word. I am going to tell it like it is. I am going to say my husband is dead. He is dead.

Two weeks have passed since my husband died. I am sitting in the family room, in my comfortable rocking chair, and I am alone. A melancholy Celine Dion song is playing, and I am weeping. After drying my tears, I look out the window and say to God: "You haven't performed a really huge, blatant miracle in a long time, and now would be the perfect time to show the world what you are capable of. So, I think you should raise my husband from the dead. Do you realize what a witness that would be? I mean, lots of people loved my husband and you would make a really big impact by bringing him back. Just bring him back and let him walk through the front door. Just bring him back. If you do not want him to simply walk through the front door, I would be happy to go to the cemetery and pick him up."

I tell God the plot numbers where Sandro is buried, just to make sure He gets the right man. Then with a sob, I bury my face in my hands.

He is not coming back, not ever. He is dead. He is Dead. *DEAD.*

I am keeping a journal. Four weeks after my husband died, I wrote: *"Four weeks gone today. This is not getting any easier. It's getting harder, sadder, more lonely. I loved you; you loved me. You died, died, died.*

That's gone, gone, gone. Is there someone there with you? It was supposed to be you with me...forever.

Whoever decided that I wanted to do this grief thing was WRONG! I do not want to do this. Do I sound angry? *Angry,* hmmm, an interesting word. Do I feel angry with my husband for dying? Five weeks after he died my journal reads: *"How dare you die. How dare you leave me alone. How dare you leave me with all these 'things' to take care of by myself. I am not going to do the 'right' thing. I am going to do what I want, finally, and you cannot say anything! Maybe I don't want to do anything. Why should I? You died on me! You were supposed to grow old with me. You promised..."*

In the midst of my grief, I am grateful that my Uncle Pete taught me to be comfortable at cemeteries. I visit my husband at the cemetery often. It is a place for me to grieve and cry and think and remember. Most of the time I go by myself, in the evening, just before it is dark. Six weeks after my husband died, I arrive at the cemetery as the sun is setting and dusk is unfolding. My journal entry reads: *"I lay on your grave tonight. I had thought about it before, but tonight...it was quiet, dusky, and just us... and I lay on top of you and remembered. Why did you have to die? Why you.... why then...why...why...why? I miss you more than I can bear sometimes. I miss you all the time. I am so lonely for you. I am so hungry for your touch, your smile, your arms around me. How do I go on without you? When does this gut-wrenching feeling end? When does my heart stop aching for you? How am I to go on without you? How???"*

How do I explain the feeling of being raw and wounded, with oceans of tears and a fragmented heart? Of gulping and swallowing, to try and keep the grief from tearing me apart. Of so much grief, despair, pain, and loneliness that I can hardly stand it. My journal reads: *"Drowning, drowning, coming up for air. Sometimes life is just not fair."*

I want to wake up from this nightmare and be normal—just normal, not fantastic, or special, or extraordinary. Just normal.

CHAPTER

Eight

HUNTING FOR SURVIVAL

Where is it? I can't find it! I've looked everywhere! What am I going to do? It must be somewhere! I've got to find it! Slow down. Breathe. Think.

Where is my survival guide? You know, the one that was written especially for me? The one that has a table of contents filled with the topics for which I most need answers. There are guides for surviving a snow storm, for fixing your car, selecting a restaurant, finding a home, grooming a pet, even one on how to remove acrylic nails. But where is my special guide on how to survive?

I need to know when to wash my sheets, because they have my husband's smell on them, and I can't bear to think of never smelling that wonderful smell, his smell, again. I need to know if the gaping hole in my stomach will ever close. I need to know how I can guide Adam and Kevin through this. I need to know if my Dad will ever recover from the experience of being with Sandro when he died. I need to know when, how, and if, I should remove my wedding ring. I need to know when to clean out Sandro's closet and dresser. I need to know if I will always have to keep swallowing to keep my grief at bay while I go through my day. I *NEED* to know.

I would consider myself a "glass half full" kind of person. I have a positive attitude about life, and I recognize and appreciate my blessings. I am a thinker, and I try to look at things from every angle. I like to figure things out, to understand why they happen. I have been known to over-analyze things, which can drive my family a little crazy. But how do I find the reason for my husband dying? How do I understand the why of his death? How do I find the blessing, any blessing, in the midst of such anguish? Where is the "glass half full" in experiencing this kind of grief? Good grief? How can grief be good? How can grief be anything but empty?

I was at work when I got the news Sandro had died. I remember thinking that I did not want to go home. Home was never, ever, going to be the same again. If I did not go home, I could pretend that everything was okay, that nothing had really changed. But if I went home…well, then Sandro's death would be real. I would not be able to deny it. I would have to face the brutal fact that he was never going to be home with us again. Home. How could it be home without him?

In the hours and days immediately following Sandro's death, there were so many things to do, and all I wanted was my old life back. My life had changed in an instant. I had not asked for the changes. I did not want the changes. I definitely did not want the heartache, the pain, the hurt, the sorrow, the loneliness, or the journey. I had not signed up, nor volunteered, nor put my name on a list for grief boot camp. But here I was, with this agonizing "to do" list. I had to notify family members, find a mortuary, talk to the coroner, bring my husband's body back home, select a minister and church, pick out a casket, buy a cemetery plot, put together the program for Sandro's service, find pictures for his memory board, and…I had to crawl into an empty bed at night.

Every aspect of my life included Sandro. We worked together, we exercised together, and we were raising a family together. Where could I go where it wouldn't seem like he was missing? There were times that I just wanted to pull the covers over my head and stay in bed. There were times, late at night, when I pulled his favorite flannel boxers out of his dresser drawer, held them, and sobbed myself to sleep. On his side of the bed.

Yet, as time passed, I came to understand that grieving is a process, not an event. Grief is not something that you can skirt around, jump over, run away from, or ignore. It is a journey that is different for everyone. I found that I needed to tackle grief one day at a time. I had to look at the grieving process and break it down into hours, days, and weeks. Grieving is difficult. It is tiring, agonizingly painful work, but it is work that must be done if there is to be true healing. So I made up my mind to square my shoulders and meet grief head on.

In the beginning all I was able to do was survive. I was the definition of survival. I was living longer than. I was enduring. I had sons to guide through grief and companies to sustain. I had responsibilities that had to be met. And every morning, when I walked into the front yard to get the newspaper, I got mad. I should not have to be picking up the morning paper. That's Sandro's job. Sandro always picked up the morning newspaper; it was part of his ritual. *Was*, past tense, the operative word.

My journey through grief was like waves crashing upon the shore. Some waves were gentle, and some so brutal that I thought I would be torn apart. I learned to lean into those waves, because I could not deny them and survive. I leaned into them, while they washed over me, and then subsided. I found that preparation was helpful. The more I could prepare with prayer and reasoning, the less I lost my footing. I also found that some days caught me totally by surprise. Those days were wipeouts. There is one thing that must be remembered about both waves and feelings of grief…you must accept them as they come. You cannot control them.

Death is so final, yet it also brings so many firsts. Firsts without your loved one. The first year is so very hard. It is the first time you experience each holiday, birthday, anniversary, important firsts in your children's lives, and maybe even the first time you have to take the car in for an oil change. Firsts hurt! My journal entry tells this story: *"One month tomorrow, 11 more months of firsts. Oh, God, help me through this, please…"*

In my hunt for survival, I learned that if I listened carefully, I had the answers inside of me. I learned to trust my instinct. To wait until it felt right. I learned that if I listened to my heart, I would know. You see, grief is also a teaching journey. As you travel through it, you have the opportunity to heal and to grow. Four months after my husband died my journal entry reads: *"Oh, how I want you back, but I want to keep the things I've learned, and come to understand, too. I know that there are hard days ahead of me… but for now, I count my blessings and I cherish the impact you, and our love, had on my life."*

Sandro was very fit, five-feet, ten-inches tall, with broad shoulders and strong arms. He loved to have me rest my head on his shoulder. Then he would wrap his arms around me, and hold me close. Recalling that simple, intimate gesture used to make my eyes fill with tears. The pain of knowing I would never experience his arms around me again sliced into me, taking my breath away. Then one day, about seven months after he died, I was at the cemetery. I was washing his headstone and trimming the grass around it. As I was carefully cleaning the dust out of the writing on his stone, I was remembering how much he loved to have my head resting on his shoulder, and I was smiling. Grief has taught me, that for the rest of my life, there will be days, hours, or moments of sadness…and that just has to be okay. But grief has also shown me that the memories that used to bring tears of sadness can now bring a smile to my face.

It has been said that a life stretched by grief never returns to its original shape. I found this to be true. But during my hunt for survival, I also found hope and faith, peace and grace, love and truth. Even in grief, the potential for growth is abundant.

CHAPTER

Nine

WHO'S IN MY CLOSET?

What are you doing in there? What are you doing here? What are you doing? I am not really sure what is going on. It is seven months since Sandro died and there he is, standing in the closet with his underwear on and his hands on his hips, looking disgusted. I don't understand.

Two days ago, I finally cleaned out Sandro's closet and drawers. It had never seemed right to do it before, but that day—seven months, two days after his death—it felt right. In the months following his death, looking at his clothes hanging in our closet in their normal, orderly fashion was a mixed blessing. Our closet was a vivid and daily reminder that while things appeared normal, they simply were not. Yet, it was comforting to have his clothes there. He used to wear them. I could still picture him in them. I could remember the places he had worn them. And, I could wear his shirts and sweatshirts when I needed to feel him next to me. Some days I just felt better with one of his sweatshirts on.

Well-meaning friends would ask if I had boxed-up his clothing yet. They seemed to believe that it was an important step in letting go, of accepting his death. I would just smile, and shake my head no. They would raise an eyebrow, and nod their head yes, like they understood. Then in my head I would scream at them, *"What do you know? Nothing. You know absolutely nothing!"* But I would hear myself telling them softly, "I'm not ready yet." Sometimes I think I should have let my head say what it thought.

Then, one beautiful March day, I woke up and knew it was time.

Not because I had to do it, but because it was just time. I had already taken his previously worn shirts and slacks to the cleaners, and they were hanging in the plastic cleaner bags. Instead of boxing them up, I had decided to give them to an organization that I trusted. I made the call to Farm Drive, a wonderful outreach ministry that our church supported, and asked if they would be interested in some men's clothing, shoes and belts. I told them that everything was cleaned and pressed, and in wonderful condition. Sandro was quite particular about his clothes, and if I was going to pass them on, I had to make sure they were immaculate. The Farm Drive director told me they would be delighted to get them. I hung up the phone and began to prepare them for a new home.

I was not going to give all of his clothes away. I wanted to make sure that each of the children had some of his clothing. I'm not sure exactly why I did that. I think I just wanted them to have something that their dad used to wear. Maybe as they grew they would try on his shoes to see if they filled them. Maybe they would wear one of his belts someday. Maybe it was my way of trying to keep him alive.

I kept the clothes he died in. When the mortuary gave them to me, they were sealed in a plastic bag. It took me months and months to open that bag, and when I did two things imprinted onto my heart. The mortuary had washed, and neatly folded, his socks, underwear and jeans. Sandro would have liked that. And the shirt he had been wearing, a forest green T-shirt, had been cut down the middle. The paramedics that had arrived first on the scene, in a medical helicopter, had cut his shirt to attach electrodes to his chest. I know, because when I picked up his shirt to hold it, there was one electrode still attached to the inside of his shirt. Ohhh, seeing that hurt. I gently put his clothes back in the bag, sealed it, and held it tightly to my chest. Then I placed the bag in a cupboard so I would know where it was, but not have to see it everyday.

When Adam and Kevin got home from school, they found me preparing to load Sandro's clothes into the Suburban so I could deliver them to Farm Drive. They told me they would take them. I remember telling them they didn't have to do that; I was okay. They assured me that it was something they both wanted to do. I looked at them closely, then nodded, and told them thank you. I believe they were trying to protect me from something they thought might be hard for me. I needed to let them do that. I also believe that it was something they wanted to do for Sandro. So the three of us loaded the Suburban, and I watched as my sons drove out of the driveway with Sandro's clothes.

Two days after his clothes were delivered to Farm Drive, I went to bed sometime after midnight. It worked best for me to go to bed when I was really tired, because it made it easier to fall asleep. The next thing I know Sandro is standing in the closet, in his underwear, and he is asking me where his clothes have gone. I try and explain to him that he doesn't need clothes anymore. He just looks at me like I'm crazy, and tells me of course he needs his clothes. He is irritated that his clothes are not there. What have I done with them, he wants to know. Where are his clothes? He looks really funny standing there in his underwear, and I start to smile at him. I'm thinking to myself, *"Doesn't he know he does not need clothes anymore? Doesn't he know that he's dead?"* It is so great to see him, he looks really good, and then it dawns on me…he does not realize he is dead.

How do you convince someone they are dead? But here I am, calmly explaining to Sandro that he does not need clothes anymore because he died. I have to tell him several times, in different ways. I see him look at me, with his cute, sheepish smile, as I wake from my dream.

CHAPTER

Ten

365 DAYS

As the first anniversary of Sandro's death approached, I tried to prepare myself. I knew I would be spending time at the cemetery that day and I wanted to take some special things with me. I began to put together a basket of items. I included my journal, some books that held special meaning for me, a small book of prayers, a blanket to sit on, and a card for him that I wanted to leave at the cemetery.

I also decided to make a card to send to the people that loved and cared for Sandro. So one beautiful, clear day I drove to the cemetery with bunches of pink and white carnations. I placed them around Sandro's headstone and took photographs. His headstone is very special to my family because Kevin designed it. It is a granite stone with the sun setting behind majestic mountains, eagles soaring, deer grazing, and my husband's favorite car, his Porsche, driving on a winding road into the sunset. I used my photograph of the headstone for the front of the card, and inside I wrote, "One year...we remember..."

And 365 days after my husband died, I sat on his grave and I remembered. I remembered his smile and his laughter. His broad shoulders and his strong arms, his walk, and the way he would wink at me when we shared a secret look. I remembered his life and his death, and I thanked God for bringing him into my life, and for the wonderful years we had together. I celebrated my husband. I told him I loved him and that I would always love him. I promised him that he would forever be a part of my life, a part of who I am.

I read my journal and wrote about the day. I smiled, I laughed, I cried…and I remembered God's promise of hope and a future. Then I thanked Him for all of the wonderful blessings He bestowed on me. I thanked Him for my sons and my family, for good friends, for being with me on my journey through grief, and for what I had learned. I thanked God for my life.

Grieving did not end for me that day, but I did celebrate that I had made it through one year of firsts.

CHAPTER
Eleven
MY TWO SONS

Adam was six when Kevin was born, and there seemed to be an immediate bond between them. When Kevin was an infant, Adam used to hold him gently in his arms while he rocked in his child-size rocking chair. From the time Kevin was one, Adam would hold him in his lap and read to him. It always made my heart smile to watch the two of them with each other. Then one day when Kevin was in kindergarten I walked into the family room and saw a familiar, but slightly different, scene. Adam was holding Kevin in his lap, but Kevin was reading to Adam. Their relationship continued to grow stronger and deeper as they got older. I have always been grateful for the close bond that they share.

I love being a mom to boys. I will admit to not always understanding them. I remember when they hit middle school years and were so excited about gaining five pounds. Personally I could not wrap my head around that, but hey they were thrilled so I was thrilled. As they grew up we tried to make memories and start traditions. When they were in high school one tradition we began was for me to take each of them to visit the colleges they were interested in attending.

The summer before Adam's senior year in high school we took a road-trip to check out colleges in southern California, just the two of us. We had an absolutely great time. It was so much fun to navigate our way around areas we were unfamiliar with, and touring the different colleges was really interesting. It was especially fun to watch Adam as he soaked up the information and enjoyed the atmosphere at each college we toured. After our road-trip I was fairly confident that when he graduated from high school he would be heading to a college in southern California. Then suddenly, six weeks after our trip, eleven months before Sandro died, Adam decided to attend San Jose State University. He wanted to study business and SJSU certainly had a good business school, but I was surprised by his choice to stay local. We discussed it, but Adam was certain he wanted to attend SJSU.

We did not have a crystal ball. We did not know what was coming. We did not know that Sandro would die within the year. But I am eternally grateful that Adam made the decision to attend SJSU.

Two years after Sandro died, Adam did move to southern California to go to school. As part of the application process he was required to write a personal essay. I asked him if I could share part of his essay with the readers of this book and he replied, "Of course!"

In Adam's words:

"My college experience began at San Jose State University. During my two years at this university, I learned a lot about myself and the type of learning environment I would need to successfully complete my education.

"My second day at San Jose State University my stepfather died suddenly and unexpectedly. He was the man who had raised me, who I thought of as my father, who I loved, admired, and looked up to. Losing him affected me profoundly. I am the oldest of two boys and my little brother, my mom and I had so much to deal with and adjust to. One thing that my mom said she was absolutely sure of was that my dad wanted me to graduate from college and he was so proud of the direction I was heading. Quitting was not an option, but it was a challenge to adjust to both university life and life without my dad."

Like most moms, I have learned many things from my children through the years. After Sandro died, each of my sons taught me something especially valuable. From Adam I learned strength. I watched as he continued to push through all the changes and challenges that come with a first semester of college. I wondered how, in the midst of such sorrow, he could go on. But he did. And he also made sure that he was always there for his little brother, always.

Well Adam did it! The day of his graduation, with family and extended family cheering him on, Adam received his bachelor's degree in business. When his name was called I cheered, and clapped, and cried. I remembered how his college years had begun. I remembered what he had gone through and how hard he had worked. I looked at his smile as he walked back to his seat from the podium, and I remember thinking, you did it Adam, you did it!

Kevin taught me acceptance. Middle school years are not easy for anyone, and Kevin was just about to start seventh grade when Sandro died. Two months after our loss we were driving to get some frozen yogurt. I had just picked him up from school and we were talking about his day. I remember, so clearly, that it was an overcast day. As our light turned green, and I made the turn, I said to him, "You seem to be doing so well. How do you handle it all?" He calmly looked at me and said, "I can tell you in one word. Acceptance."

Five years after Sandro died it was Kevin's turn for a road trip to visit colleges and then begin the application process. For one of his applications he also had to write a personal essay. When I asked him if I could share parts of his essay he replied, "That is totally fine!"

In Kevin's words:

"One of the hardest things for people to face is death. The loss of a loved one is one of the most unthinkable and undesirable situations. No one wants to face sudden death, and no one expects it. Yet, it is something that we all have to deal with. About five years ago my stepdad passed away. He went away for a one-day hunting trip, and we had no idea anything would go wrong. That afternoon we learned that he had suffered a heart attack, and that he did not make it. This event left my mom, my older brother, and myself on our own again. He was not just a stepfather to me. He was the biggest, and only father figure in my life because I did not see my real dad that often. I was very attached to him, and I called him dad.

Most of the values I have learned, I learned from my mom. For a while she was the only parent I knew. People say that a child learns love from the mother, and strength from the father. I definitely got a lot of love from my mom and if you were to ask anyone if I am a strong person, they would emphatically say yes. This is because my mom is one of the strongest people I know, and from her I got my strength as well. One of the major reasons that my family got through the death of my stepdad is because my mom pulled us through it. She always made sure we were all right, even when she was probably the one who needed comforting.

I have always looked up to my brother, Adam. He is probably the greatest brother anyone could have. Even when I was small, he was always willing to do things with me. While other brothers were fighting, we were getting along and sharing many common hobbies. My stepdad's death was one of the few times that I saw my brother cry. This was unusual for me because he was always the big, older brother. What he taught me was that it is okay for boys to let their guard down, that boys do not always have to be tough, and that everyone has real emotions that need to be dealt with.

New ideas and new situations are presented to us everyday. It is our responsibility to determine what is learned from our experiences. Are we going to just sit there and feel sorry for ourselves, or are we going to try and make the best of the situation that we have been given. Personally, I like to make the best of a situation so that I can learn from it."

I am so blessed by my sons. I am still amazed at the love, support, and strength each of them exhibited at such a painful time in their lives. As I prepared this chapter and read their college essays once again, I was reminded of the wonderful boys they were and the amazing men they have become.

CHAPTER

Twelve

LIFELINES: GRAB ON, HOLD TIGHT

I will always remember…It was one of those "aha!" moments. Within 48 hours of Sandro's death, I knew I was glad to be alive. I remember sitting in the family room, curled up in my favorite rocking chair, and feeling painfully sad about losing Sandro and yet incredibly grateful that I was alive. Somehow, through the haze of the initial days of loss, hope was shining through. I grabbed hold of that sliver of hope and held on tight.

My sons, Adam and Kevin, were my reasons for getting up every morning. All I had to do was look at them, or think of them, to know that hope existed for me. I am not really sure how or why, but I knew immediately that I did not want my sons to feel they had to take care of me. That was a burden I was not going to let them carry. I believed that it was my job to help them cope with their loss, and to encourage them to embrace their feelings of grief, anger, and pain. I did not want my sons to gloss over any part of their grieving process because I did not want them to carry the burden of unfinished grief with them for the rest of their lives. At their tender ages of 18 and 12, I knew the devastating loss of Sandro would have considerable impact on the men they would become. I wanted that impact to be compassion, sensitivity, and consideration for others experiencing loss. I wanted them to feel secure in the knowledge that they had not only survived; they had thrived.

I returned to work just seven days after Sandro's death. I parked in the back of the building, and got out of my car. With my keys in my hand, and my briefcase over my shoulder, I started walking towards the door. When I got to the door I stopped, took a deep breath and looked down, trying to gather my courage to unlock the door and walk through it. It was then that I noticed I was wearing one black shoe and one navy-blue shoe, same style, definitely different colors.

What a dork, I thought. Shaking my head I smiled, unlocked the door and walked into the building. Something I had so dreaded had been made easier because of a shoe mix-up.

People do not always know what to say to someone who is grieving. Sometimes they say thoughtless, unthinking, or unkind things. Forty-eight hours after I found out Sandro had died, I was told by a co-worker/friend that I looked terrible. She was probably right, but I just wanted to scream. How did she expect me to look? Then there was the person who told me that my sons were lucky, that at least their "real" father hadn't died. There was that urge to scream again. I will make sure I don't pass those words onto my sons. At first some of these comments stung me. I was stunned that people would say such things. I quickly learned to dismiss these types of comments, to just let them go. Compared to death, they held little impact. I have to believe that these words and questions were not said to be intentionally cruel or hurtful. They just did not know any better. I promised myself that I would learn from this, that I would know better. I would learn to pass on comfort.

Cards and phone messages. Both of these were so important to me. They meant that Sandro was not forgotten. They meant that people cared that he was gone. Every day, when I came home from work, I went to the mailbox. When I saw that there were sympathy cards, I had such mixed feelings. I was so grateful that someone cared, and so sad that they were coming to me. I just didn't want to be the one that needed to get a sympathy card. Yet, I didn't want these notes to stop coming, because I thought that would mean that no one remembered my husband anymore. I felt the same way about the phone messages. Both the cards and the phone messages eventually slowed to a trickle, then they stopped. I understood, and understand, why. I know that even though we did not have normal, other people did. I was especially grateful for the lone card that still appeared in my mailbox on occasion. Someone letting me know that we were in their thoughts. I decided that when someone I knew was grieving, I would be that person who sent a card weeks or months later. I would let them know I remembered.

One autumn day, three months after Sandro died, I was walking though the park with my "straight-talking" friend, Debby. I was berating myself for not knowing that he was going to die. For not, somehow, being able to do something that would have made him NOT die. I said to Debby, "I should have known. I should have been able to do something." She stopped in her tracks, turned, looked at me and firmly stated, "So you're saying you killed him." I looked at her, shocked, and quickly said, "Of course, I didn't kill him."

"You're right," Debby said. "You did NOT kill him."

At that moment, right then, I so needed her brutal honesty. I needed my heart to feel what my head knew. My friend's honesty helped me get there.

The evening before Valentine's Day hit, I was wondering how I was going to get through it. The year before Sandro had surprised me with a beautiful birthstone ring that was wrapped in (and I'll tell you if you promise not to tell a soul) a bright red, lacy, one-piece teddy. This year, I was getting a card and flowers together to take to the cemetery. My shoulders slumped, my head dropped to my chest, and my heart hurt. Then, the doorbell rang. I went to answer the door, looked through the peephole, and saw my brother-in-law, Jeff. I opened the door and there he stood, with beautiful flowers and a card for me. For me. He had a card and flowers for me. I will always remember his gift of kindness and I will pass it on to others.

I had a strong desire to meet and talk to other women who had lost their husbands. I wanted to gather wisdom from them, to learn how they had made it, that they had made it. I wanted to see that there was life and living after loss and grief. Some of the women I spoke with made me sadder. It seemed like they had not completed their journey through grief, that they had gotten stuck somewhere along the path. They seemed bitter and alone and somehow separated from life. They seemed to have no hope. Other women I spoke with appeared to be running from grief as fast and as far as they could. They would say everything was just fine, couldn't be better, but their eyes told a different story. They were afraid to stop running long enough to feel. Then there were the women who spoke truth to me. Women who shared what their lives were like before their husbands had died, and since their husbands' deaths. They were honest about the relationships they had with their husbands. Not perfect, just real, normal relationships with all the emotions that loving someone brings. These women had come through grief. They had made it to the other side. They had normal again.

Twice in my life I have been asked, "Is there someone there with you?" By now you know that I believe in God. He was with me in those midnight hours when sleep wouldn't come, and the tears would flow. He was with me when I was afraid, and sad, and angry. He wasn't afraid of any of my emotions or feelings, rather I think He expected them.

There are so many different types of lifelines to hold onto when you are grieving. Grab on to the lifelines that make you feel better. Hold tight to those slivers of hope and moments of humor. Do not be afraid of any emotion. Do not be afraid to feel. Do not be afraid. You will make it through.

CHAPTER
Thirteen
AFTERSHOCKS AND THE GLOBAL WORRIER

After an earthquake, there may be aftershocks. Aftershocks are a reminder of the traumatic event, of the fact that we are not in control of when the earth decides to tremble. They can be so mild that we hardly notice them, and they may hit so violently that we think it is another "big one." They are so unsettling.

Aftershocks is the name I have given to the many feelings and emotions that have hit since Sandro's death. Some deal directly with the pain and the memories associated with his death. Others are like a residue that is left on my heart. The hardest aftershocks for me? They are the ones that hit out of the blue and play with my head.

I am a fairly intuitive person, but the day Sandro died was just a normal day for me. I had no feeling that anything was going to go wrong. I had no inclination that he was dying. I was just going about my day oblivious that life was about to change forever. Sometimes now, when a day is blissfully normal, I worry that I'm missing something. That something horrible is about to happen, or has happened, and I just don't know it yet. This is usually in regard to my family, or extended family, and that worry can turn quickly into fear and make me sick inside. A normal day turned on me once before. I don't want that to ever happen again.

You see, the biggest aftershock that I experienced, and still struggle with, is fear. You know the type of fear I mean. The kind that grips you like a vice, the kind of "look under the bed for the monster, close the closet doors when the lights are out, and don't go into the basement without a light" fear. This type of fear just sits and waits to devour you. It lies low in your sub-conscious mind and the pit of your stomach, and it waits. It waits for the opportunity to wash over you and flood you with doubts, what ifs, and "I cannot lose another loved one... ever" fear. This kind of fear can take away your freedom, rob you of your potential, and make you second-guess your decisions. It can suck you dry and turn you into someone who is afraid of even normal things, like a field trip for your child, an airplane vacation, or a missed phone call. Even when you know it's not rational, logical or reasonable, this kind of aftershock can still suffocate you.

Now I don't want you to think that I only worry about my loved ones or people I care for, because you see, I am also a global worrier. I worry about war, terrorism, disease, genocide, starvation, the elderly in convalescent hospitals, orphans...you get the picture.

I had just turned 43 when Sandro died and I believed that I would never marry again. I remember telling my sister, Ann, the day after he died, that I could live to be twice my age, which would mean that I would live half of my life alone. I had always believed that Sandro and I would grow very old together, and now he was gone. Ann in her wisdom calmly said, "Just take this one day at a time, Sally." Well, I have remarried. Steve and I have known each other since I was 15 and he was 17. We have always been able to talk and share our feelings. After we got married I told Steve how, oftentimes, I cried in the shower. The shower was my private place to let my grief out and to allow my tears to flow. I asked him to please check on me if I was ever in the shower for longer than 30 minutes, because that meant I was having a hard time. He very softly said he would. There have been several occasions where Steve has gently knocked on the door to check on me, to make sure I am okay. After all this time, the shower is still the place where I shed most of my tears.

Then, there are my sweats. Usually when I get home from work, I put my hair in a ponytail and change into sweats for the evening. In the morning, before I leave for work I always fold my sweats and put them away. Even if I am running late, I never leave my sweats out. If anything were to happen to me that day, I don't want my husband to come home and find my sweats waiting for me. Some mornings I tell myself, "It's okay, leave them out. You can't keep thinking like that. Let it go. It will be okay." But is doesn't seem to matter what I tell myself. I always fold them and put them away, just in case.

Aftershocks have had some positive effects on me as well. I have learned that life can change in a heartbeat. So I always, and this is a big ALWAYS, try to make sure that my loved ones know how much I love them and how blessed I feel that they are a part of my life. I have told them that if I were to die suddenly or young (to me, young equals anything under age 96), it would not be my choice, but that I have felt loved and truly blessed. I have also written letters to my sons and my husband. I have written to them so that when I die, they will have some final words of love from me. I want them to be able to grab onto my words, my love, my feelings, if they need to. I want them to have something tangible to hold onto. My hope is that they will hear my voice when they read the letters and will feel the love I have for them.

As I write this, it has been eight and one-half years since Sandro died. There are still moments, hours or days, when I feel unsettled and I don't know what to make of myself. There are times when I just feel incredibly sad. Sometimes it catches me by surprise, and I have to reason with myself to figure out what is wrong. Then I have one of those "aha!" moments, and I realize that grief has popped up again and I am having an aftershock.

How do you deal with aftershocks? You accept that they are a part of life after loss and when they hit, you ride them out. You learn not to be afraid to ask for help, for prayers, for words of comfort or wisdom. You lean into them, feel them, and understand they will pass. And you hold on to hope.

Jeremiah 29:11 – "For I know the plans I have for you," declares the Lord, "plans to prosper you and not to harm you, plans to give you hope and a future."

CHAPTER

Fourteen

DON'T SWEAT THE SMALL STUFF

Just when you thought you were done with me, I am back with a footnote to my story. It's really more of a reminder…

In September 2004, I had a headache on the left side of my head. I rarely get headaches, but for some reason they always seem to occur on the left side of my head. Steve rubbed my head, neck and shoulders for me, trying to work out the knots. I finally resorted to taking Ibuprofen to take the edge off, hoping that it would help enough to allow me to sleep.

The next day the left side of my neck was a bit sore. Absentmindedly, I put my fingers on the sore spot. I felt a knot, a hard, almond-shaped knot. I did a quick check on the right side of my neck to compare (hoping another knot was there so it would be "normal"). No knot on the right side. Hmmm, I thought. Should I be worried? My annual exam with my gynecologist was scheduled in two days. I would just show the knot to her. I was sure she would tell me it was from stress, or yoga, or simply a swollen lymph node from an allergy.

Well, I must have felt that knot 100 times in the two days between finding it and seeing my doctor. On the day of my exam, I told her about the knot and then showed her where it was. She felt the knot in my neck and told me that I should check with an internist because lymph nodes were not really her specialty. Then she stepped back from me and said, "If you're worried about lymphoma you would probably have other symptoms as well, like night sweats, sudden weight loss, general fatigue." She lost me on lymphoma. I asked her a few more questions, looking for reassurance that this knot of mine was nothing.

No reassurance, just a restating that I should see an internist. Wow. Not what I was expecting.

I left her office and drove to my internist's office, only two blocks away. I thought that maybe if I were physically standing in his office, they would squeeze me in and put this issue to rest. They were able to schedule an appointment for early the next morning. I was grateful, but I had another 22 hours to wait. During the night I prayed, "Please let it be nothing, God. Please let it be nothing."

I was shown into an examining room, right on time, the next morning. My blood pressure was taken and, needless to say, it was elevated (go figure!). My doctor came in, and I gave him the information on my knot. He spent several minutes feeling my neck and my knot. I was grateful he was being so thorough.

Then he said, "I'd like you to have an MRI of the mass."

My mind is shouting: What? A Mass? An MRI? I don't think so. This is just a little knot. No big deal.

My mouth politely, and calmly, said, "What's the worst case scenario? Should I freak out about this?"

He answered, "Lymphoma, but I'm not convinced it's a lymph node and, no, don't freak out. Let's just find out."

"Could I just have a biopsy?" my mouth again politely queried.

"No," he said. "It could be a tangle of blood vessels and we don't want to do anything until we know what we're dealing with."

Whoa. I did not expect this. When did my knot become a mass?

After Sandro died, I seemed to be in a grace period when the little nuisances of life did not bother me or matter much. I did not worry about the small stuff. Something big had happened to us and the little things that used to drive me crazy did not impact me at all. I remember telling myself that I would never again get caught up in the bothersome little things of life. No more obsessing over minutia for me.

Time went by and eventually I found myself being driven crazy by the little things again. I obsessed over things I could not control. Now, faced with words like lymphoma, MRI, mass…the little things do not seem to matter, again. I am afraid. I stand at the nurses' station as they call the hospital to schedule my MRI. The earliest day is six days from now. Six days. How will I manage six days?

I walk to my car and call my husband. I explain what the doctor has told me and Steve is very quiet. Then, with love in his voice, he says: "It will be okay."

I do not want to become a medical case. I want normal. My logical side is grateful for my internist's thoroughness. My emotional side is trying to control itself. Sitting in my car, I call the MRI scheduling number and ask if I can be placed on a waiting list for cancellations. Cancellations are rare, the scheduler explains. She is very kind, and I thank her for that. Kindness is important to me right now.

My usual way of dealing with something of this magnitude would be to keep it between Steve and me. I will try to handle it myself, to make sure I do not burden anyone else. But I know that I am not going to do that this time. I call my dear friend, Pattie, to talk. I hang up without telling her because "it's no big deal" and I can surely handle it myself. I end up calling Pattie back later that evening. I need reassurance. I need prayers. Frankly, I just need.

Being needy is scary. It is a vulnerable, hanging-out-there-alone-on-the-trapeze kind of feeling. But here I am sharing my fears, and my needs, with my sisters and a few close friends. The world did not stop turning because I told people, because I reached out with my neediness. Rather, I was now on the receiving end of prayers, kindnesses, gentleness, compassion, and even humor.

Steve and I talked, too, and he supported my decision not to tell Adam and Kevin, or my parents. After we had the "good news," then we would tell them. I just did not want them to worry about something that could not be controlled. Hmmm, there is that word again. Control. Yet again, I am learning a lesson about control.

My MRI was moved up one day. Please, I pray, let everything be normal. Not wonderful or extraordinary, just normal. I have prayed this prayer before.

God answered all of our prayers. The results came back within 24 hours: "No abnormal mass. No abnormal lymph nodes."

Apparently, I have a knotty neck. That's normal for me.

I am normal. I am normal! Thank you, God, for normal!

This experience reminded me, once again, that no amount of worry, or fear, or anxious and obsessive thinking accomplishes anything. I am not the one in control.

Learning to let go of worry and fear and control may be happening in baby-steps for me. But that is okay, because even baby-steps mean progress…

"Who of you by worrying can add a single hour to his life? Since you cannot do this very little thing, why do you worry about the rest?" Luke 12:25-26

Epilogue, April 2007

Psalm 30 verse 5: " . . . weeping may remain for the night, but rejoicing comes in the morning."

I am going to be a grandmother. Yes, a grandma. My oldest son, Adam, and his wonderful wife, Kate, are expecting their first child. I am thrilled, and over the moon with joy.

Kevin, my youngest son, has graduated from college and is in graduate school. He and his sweet girlfriend, Emily, have a long-distance relationship while they complete their educations.

My husband, Steve, is coaching water polo and swimming at the high school level. He loves working with the kids, and watching them grow and mature.

It has been almost eleven years since Sandro died. I do not know where the time has gone. Sometimes it still seems like the loss happened yesterday, but often it feels like I watched another person experience it a long time ago.

For me, life is full and rich and I count my blessings. In the last eleven years there have been times of joy, sadness, celebration, disappointment, excitement, worry, fulfillment, concern, and growth. You know . . . normal times.

Life can change in a heartbeat. But I know, with absolute certainty, that God is in every part of my life. From the huge moments to the smallest of details, He is there. And He cares about it all.

Acknowledgements

To my three men, Steve, Adam, and Kevin. Thank you for your unwavering love, support, and encouragement as I traveled first through grief, then tackled this monster of an endeavor. You are my anchors.

To my parents, Ed and Jean Stangohr, your unconditional love helped sustain me. Mom, thank you for your constant prayers, your sensitive heart, and your quiet understanding. Dad, thank you for always being there; you held Sandro's hand as he died and held mine as I fought to survive.

To my sisters, Ann and Sandy, I thank you for your unyielding love. You circled the wagons to care for me in every imaginable way. Thank you to my brothers-in-law Jeff and Tim, my nephews Seth, Josh, and Ben, and my niece Katie. You are all part of my hope.

My family, I want you all to know, you are my piece of heaven right here on earth…

Thank you to Sandro's family. Even in the midst of your own grief, you offered much welcomed support during the hardest of times.

I offer heartfelt thanks to my friend, Laurie Duckham-Shoor, for her caring, wisdom, and guidance in both my initial days of loss and for the months following.

I am ever grateful to the following compassionate people who knew just how to help: The coroner from San Luis Obispo County, the Chapel of the Hills mortuary staff, and Gary from Madronia Cemetery.

Many thanks to my friend, Chris Camor, and to my aunt, Martha Carol Shelton, for their hours of thoughtful reading, loving suggestions, and unlimited enthusiasm.

For their brave hearts, faithfulness, friendship, and loving snaps, I thank my co-authors Pattie and Heather. This story, finally written, would not have existed without them.

To all who offered support, prayers, grocery shopping, food, cards, phone calls, listening hearts, and hope…I am forever grateful.

With love,

Sally

Los Gatos, California
December 20, 2005

Pattie's STORY

To my
MOM.
Your prayers and love have sustained me through life.
Thank you for being my biggest cheerleader.
I love you.

CHAPTER

One

BREAST CANCER AND KITCHEN ANTS

*T*ruth be told, my idea of a perfect Saturday would be to wake before the sun and without the aid of my alarm clock. I would lie still, then eventually I'd roll over to peek at the clock and realize that there was nowhere I needed to be that day. No pressing meeting, no reason to push me from the coziness of my bed and the rhythmic sounds of my husband's breathing.

My perfect day would include shuffling through recipe books, looking for something new to try and ending up with a tasty treat that required chocolate as the primary ingredient. At some point in the day I would team up with my husband Brian, and we would stroll through the garden section of Orchard Supply Hardware. I would spend the day working in my yard and sweeping the front porch. When I would finally glance at my watch, I'd be shocked that it was already 4:30 p.m. Time slips by. Brian and I would head to the grocery store to pick up items for a barbeque, and we'd set the table to match the number of kids and friends who happened by. We would eat out on the patio because it would be just the right kind of weather. No one would be in a hurry. We would laugh and talk and enjoy the last warmth of the sun.

The air would eventually turn cool. The dessert (with chocolate, of course) would be sweet. And the coffee, hot. We would head into our living room to conquer the big question of the night: "What DVD should we watch?" And we would come to the same conclusion we always do, our perennial top choice, "What About Bob?" My kids would make bets as to how long it will take me to fall sound asleep under my warm blanket. Like any perfect Saturday, I would not disappoint them.

A normal day. Nothing glitzy or glamorous about it. Normal. The crazy thing about "normal" is we come to expect it. Maybe even feel we deserve it. But having normal taken away from us —losing normal—makes us long for it even more.

At 42, I was diagnosed with breast cancer. My normal life? Put on hold. Nothing about my life was normal now. Life felt strangely un-normal.

When you go through crisis and loss you can't really imagine that you can have a "normal" day ever again. A day when you aren't consumed by the sadness that has come knocking. A few days after my diagnosis, I remember talking with a friend who had experienced breast cancer. She said: "Pattie, I know you can't imagine it right now, but a day is coming when you won't be obsessed with thoughts of breast cancer. Life will return to normal and, believe it or not, the biggest complaint of the day will be the fact that you have ants in your kitchen."

I listened to my friend's words and thought, "Oh, how I long for ants in my kitchen."

––––––––

Ever bite off more than you can chew? Tackle something that is W-A-Y bigger than you originally thought? That's the way I live my life, taking on a challenge without much thought of the details involved.

I remember one day in particular. I was shopping at Home Depot for the sole purpose of buying impatiens for my yard. As I entered the store my eye caught the most intriguing sign. Hmmm. Sod on sale … for just a few dollars a roll! I immediately pictured that dry patch of dirt in the front of my house next to the curb. Instantly, I was excited. I asked the man in the orange apron, "How involved would it be to lay down sod?" He said there really wasn't that much to it. Basically, you roll out the grass and water it. That's all I needed to hear. I was going to have a world-class lawn by the end of the day! I loaded my minivan and away I went with high hopes of lush lawn.

As with many of my "inspirations," they tend to end up with my husband pulled in to "help." But this time, Brian would be equally excited by my big bargain and how EASY it was going to be. After all, the guy at Home Depot, the lawn expert, said you just roll the grass out and water it. How hard could this be?

As I drove into my driveway, a smile of contentment upon my face, my eye caught that "dry patch" that I had pictured quite differently at the store. At the store it didn't have all those weeds and I did not remember the soil being so clay-like and rock hard. My excitement waned. But just a bit. I unloaded the sod and piled it in the garage thinking to myself, "I have three hours before Brian gets home from his back-packing trip. Won't he be surprised? And EXCITED!" Ohhh, he was excited. Little did I know, the Home Depot guy left out some rather important details. Like the need to pull weeds, to rent a tiller, and to buy a special tool to press the sod into place. He also failed to mention how many hours this job might actually take. It seemed so easy when he said, "Just roll out the grass and water it." I should have known.

I'm an upbeat and generally all-around happy person. Some might even call me perky. It's true. I tend to go through most days with a smile on my face. I love to laugh and I try to find the humor in most situations. Take the story of my friend's bridal shower, for instance. My good friend Debbie was hosting a bridal shower for a mutual friend. I received an invitation in the mail and quickly called with my RSVP. I made a mental note that the shower was on Tuesday. I had a full day and was running late. With time ticking away, I wrapped the shower gift, quickly said good-bye to my kids and ran out the front door. If I hurried, I would be only 10 minutes late. I pulled into my friend's neighborhood and was surprised to find such ample parking. I grabbed my gift, shut the car door and ran up the front steps of her home (still enthused about my "princess parking" spot). I knocked on the front door. In the few moments it took for the door to be opened, a thought crossed my mind: *"Hmmm, how strange that there are no lights on in the front of the house."*

Footsteps approached the front door. My friend's husband opened the door. And there we stood, mouths hanging open, looking rather inquisitively at one another.

"The shower's not tonight, is it?" I asked.

Nope, not that kind of shower. No bridal shower tonight.

The bridal shower was scheduled for Wednesday night, not Tuesday. After a briefly embarrassing visit, I handed over my gift and told my friend I would be back the next night. After laughing at myself (joined by her husband and entire family, of course), I climbed back into my car and thought to myself, "What a disappointment. I am having such a good hair day!"

Laughter. It has the ability to pull together complete strangers, unite families, and keep friendships strong. It's what allows us to show our humanness. It's fairly easy, however, to live life with a smile on your face, and laughter in your heart, when your biggest issues are sod and showing up 24 hours early to a party. It's easy to have that "can do" attitude, to be the cheerleader and see the glass half full when life's challenges are not life threatening or heartbreaking. The big test is how one faces life when it comes crashing down. My crash hit in May 2002.

I remember the phone call well. Actually, I was expecting it. The results of my breast biopsy would be in that day. It is nearly impossible to prepare yourself for a moment like this, even though I had already gone through every possible scenario in my mind. In the span of a five-minute phone conversation, my life changed forever.

I remember standing in my kitchen next to my fridge where my phone sits. This is a place where I have shared many happy conversations. I had stood in the exact spot and received phone calls from dear friends with familiar voices. Many times I would pick up the phone and hear my husband say, "Don't cook tonight, Pat, we're going out." On that phone and in that spot I heard my children's voices calling to let me know they arrived safely at their destination.

But not that day. That day there would be a strange voice with unwanted and unwelcome news. I remember grabbing a piece of paper and a pen and writing down words like *lumpectomy, radiation, DCIS cells, and mastectomy.* The voice on the other end of the phone gave me the name of a cancer website.

I remember writing down the date of my next appointment and my surgeon's name. And as I hung up the phone I thought to myself, "I have a surgeon?"

CHAPTER
Two
ADMISSION INTO CLUB LOSS

When I was a little girl, I never heard the word cancer. Oh, I knew what cancer was, but it didn't have anything to do with *my* life. Cancer happened to people far away, not to the people in my neighborhood or in my school, and certainly not in my family. Getting the flu bug for a week was about the worst it got in my family. I grew up strong and healthy, with no thoughts that my health would ever be an issue.

When I was in junior high, our family received its first health scare. My mom had to go in for a breast biopsy. That was the first time that the word cancer had made its way into my family's home. I was frightened by the thought of my mother being sick, so I did the only thing I could think of. I made a deal with God.

My family and I attended a little Baptist church near our home and I was involved in the junior high youth group. I had heard about a speech contest that was scheduled in a few weeks and I instantly made a promise to God. I told God I would enter the speech contest if He would spare my mom from cancer. I entered the contest and, much to my happiness, my mom's biopsy was fine. I thought to myself, "Aha! I made a deal with God." Little did I know, I was buying into a lie, a big, fat lie that made me feel like I could be in control when bad things happened. And all I had to do is make a deal with God.

It wasn't until I was 42 years old and facing the biggest disappointment of my life that I realized the magnitude of the lie I had believed in all those years. As I would soon discover, there is no deal to be made. No pact to be brokered with God. Through dark days and pain I would learn that I don't have that kind of power. I would also learn the beauty of God's plan.

The two weeks following my initial phone call from Dr. Yoon were torture. There were so many unknowns ahead. I played the "What if ...?" game daily. I would think about every possible scenario, *"What if this happens or that happens?"* I lived in a constant state of fear. Oh, I got up every morning and made my bed and put a smile on my face, but inside I was tormented by my own darkest thoughts, my "What If ...."

My official diagnosis was *Ductal Carcinoma Insitu* (DCIS, for short.) DCIS means that the cancer cells are inside the ducts but have not spread through the walls of the ducts into the surrounding breast tissue. Dr. Yoon explained to me that the next step would be a lumpectomy. The goal would be to surgically remove the cancer cells, get a clear radius of healthy cells around it and move on with my life. I stepped into that surgery with high hopes of being able to keep my breast.

Waiting is the worst part of any medical problem. After my surgery, I had several days until I would meet with my surgeon for the results. My thoughts grew more and more morose and fearful during this waiting period. I entered into what I would call a cold, dark cave.

The cave represents a place where I could run to when life was overwhelming me. The cave was an unhealthy place for me. Oh, at first the cave seems like it might offer some safety and protection. In reality, it brought isolation and restriction. I had taken several steps into the cave of fear. As I stepped into the cave and took a deep breath, the air was stagnate and musty. As I walked, I could feel the dirt crunch beneath my feet.

If I wasn't visiting the cave of fear, I was spending time in other caves, like the "What If Cave" or the "Cave of Hopelessness and Despair." As I spent time in these caves my mind went to thoughts about my future, or the lack of a future. What if it's worse than they thought? What if I have to have chemo? People get sick from chemo. I don't want to have chemo. I've heard radiation makes your skin burn, this could be so painful. And what if I lose my hair? I love my hair. I finally can wear my hair in a ponytail. I love wearing my hair in a ponytail. It makes me feel young.

I feel so old. What if I lose my breast? I hate the word mastectomy. I hate the way it rolls off my tongue. I hate the way it is pronounced and I hate the idea of being forced to join THAT club of women. You know the club I'm talking about. We read their stories in women's magazines, and hear about their journeys on Oprah. "Women who have lost their breasts, next on Oprah…." Mastectomy. Oh, I hated that word.

How will my kids react to the news? How will breast cancer affect my family? Who will cook dinner tonight? Who will cook dinner next week? Next month? How can I make love with my husband with just one breast? Day and night these thoughts haunted me as I stepped farther into my caves.

The news I would receive from Dr. Yoon pushed me back into my caves, especially the dark cave of despair. I remember sitting in Dr. Yoon's office with my husband when the doctor walked in. She looked at us and said, "Well, I have good news and bad news." (These, by the way, are not really the words you want to hear from your surgeon.) "The good news: We were able to get all the early-cancer cells and we got a good radius of healthy cells around it."

"Wait a minute!" I wanted to scream. "Wasn't that our goal?"

Dr. Yoon went on to explain that the bad news was there was more than one area in the breast affected with DCIS cells (Multi-Focal). The doctor said they would come back, much more aggressively.

At that moment, any control that I thought I might still have evaporated. The doctor's next sentence: "Your next step is a mastectomy."

CHAPTER
Three

WHERE ARE ALL THE HURTING PEOPLE?

The day I was given the news from my doctor, I remember being told to stop by the nurse's station on the way out. Such a simple statement. I figured that I had to pick up the card for my next appointment. Instead, the nurse went to a special file drawer and pulled out a one-inch thick packet titled, "Breast Cancer Portfolio." As she dropped it into my hands it felt as if the weight of the world was held in that packet. The packet felt thick and awkward and I certainly did not want to hold it. Just carrying that portfolio was a signal to everyone in the waiting room that I was a new member of the Breast Cancer Club. This was not the Girl Scouts of America. No, we didn't get to wear cute green uniforms. We carried one-inch thick white portfolios.

As I left, I scanned the room to see if any other women were carrying the dreaded white folder. Any other women with breast cancer? Any other women being dragged into club membership, kicking and screaming? Where are all the hurting people?

I threw the packet onto my bed when I got home. I let it sit there most of the day and well into the evening, until I finally got the courage to open it. The folder was jammed full of pamphlets, booklets, and phone numbers for support groups. Oh, great! Now I'm going to need a support group? My thought: There's another club to avoid.

As I pulled the pamphlets out, I read some pretty alarming statistics. One in nine women are diagnosed with breast cancer each year. In the state of California alone, 20,000 women are diagnosed each year. Those numbers scared me. But at the same time, they did bring me some comfort. I wasn't alone after all. There were other women out there hurting as much as me. Other women who were crawling into bed next to their husbands, scared to death just like me. As I rested my head on Brian's back, I became so aware of how naturally both breasts rested there as well. My thoughts quickly went to, *"How strange it will feel, to have only one breast rest against Brian's back."* My sad thoughts released the tears that had been threatening to emerge all day. The wetness between my check and his back caused him to roll over and embrace me with his big, strong arms.

A member of the club, and yet so alone. Isn't there supposed to be a president of this club? A secretary or treasurer? You know, the other members of the club? One in nine. Where are they?

I remember going to the mall before my mastectomy and looking at the people passing me by. Watching other women with their hands full of packages, laughing with their girlfriends, whizzing past me without so much as a glance or smile. I thought to myself, *"Well, they certainly don't have breast cancer!"* At times I wanted to scream at the top of my lungs: "Does anyone else here have breast cancer? Anyone?"

Each time I pass by a woman who is alone and walking slowly, like me, I think, *"Does she have breast cancer, too? Is she doing the same thing I am? Is she trying to pass the time and get her mind off the 'C' word?"*

Where are all the hurting people? Is she at home trying to make it through another day? Is she too weary to find her car keys and drag her broken heart out into the public? If I knew where she lived, I would go ring her doorbell. When she answered the door I would reach out and hug her and tell her that I am scared, too.

But I do not know her address, so I can't ring her bell. So I continue to walk the mall alone, fooling everyone I pass, like I'm just another shopper. In reality, I am broken into a million pieces and looking for a cave, a little escape.

CHAPTER
Four
I DON'T WANT TO DO THIS ANYMORE!

People say the dumbest things. I think you are especially aware of it when your heart, or body, is broken. I remember one day a man I barely knew spotted me in a crowd of people. He approached me and the first words out of his mouth were, "Is it true?"

I responded, "Is what true?"

"Do you have cancer?" he asked.

I replied. "Yes, I do."

At that moment I wanted to be ANYWHERE but talking to him. He continued (those kind always do), "Well, we better say good-bye to that blonde hair of yours."

His words hit me like a punch to the gut. The kind of hit that crosses your eyes and knocks the breath out of you. I wanted to scream, "I don't want to do this anymore, God! I want my old life back."

I hated being pitied.

I hated being connected with the phrase, "Did you hear about Pattie?"

I was tired of being consumed by thoughts of breast cancer. And I did not want to stand in front of the mirror one more time and try to imagine what I will look like with my left breast missing.

One of the most annoying things about crisis and loss is that life continues. Life moves on. People around me moved forward with their lives. Friends were going on vacations, planning parties, having babies, and getting engaged. You know, all the good stuff in life. And there I was.

It seemed like only yesterday; I was exactly like my friends. I was the one planning the parties, going on vacation and celebrating life. Now, it felt like the only things written on my calendar were doctors' appointments and my surgery date.

Reality has a way of slapping you in the face. As the days passed, and the truth of my situation was becoming clear to me, I dreaded the future. I was discouraged when I thought about all the difficult hurdles ahead of me. I still understood that God had a plan for me. I just hated the plan.

And I was beginning to despise the word acceptance. After all, what does that word really mean? That this is the way it is? No turning back?

No turning back ever? You mean I can't go back to life before weekly doctor appointments and blood tests? Before plastic surgeons and biopsies? I can never go back to that carefree life I used to live? Even on Saturdays?

This is not the life I signed up for. I signed up for the life where I grow old with my husband. Where I meet girlfriends for dinner and the biggest complaint of the day is the long line at the car wash. We linger over dessert because the laughter from friends is so addicting. We reminisce about how our bodies looked in our 20s, and laugh about sagging breasts and bigger butts. That's the life I signed up for! Not a life where, at the same dinner, conversation is strained. There are awkward pauses because even friends don't know what to say and no one really likes to talk about breast cancer.

It takes awhile for shocking news to settle in. When the word mastectomy was first spoken to me, with my name attached to it, it was like the word hung in the air above me. It is as if I could see that word and the phrasing around it, vibrating and bouncing off the walls around me. And there I was, standing in the middle of the room, shielding my heart. Putting my hand up over my chest, my breasts, as if to say I will not allow entrance into my life. But there was that moment when I had to take my hand off my heart, off my chest, and let the truth settle in.

I guess you could call it acceptance. Acceptance came into my life rather gently. It did not come with the force of a bulldozer. Slowly, God showed me that He had a plan for me. This wasn't just some random bad thing that was happening to me. Over time, I have come to embrace the crisis instead of hiding from it or trying to protect myself from it.

Twenty-one days before my mastectomy, I wrote in my journal on July 8, 2002: *"Today I say NO to cancer and YES to life."*

CHAPTER
Five
DARKNESS OF DESPAIR

I hate delays! Just when I want to move forward, everything halts. I have a good friend who also suffers from a "Type A, run 500 mph, don't stop 'til you're finished" personality. She puts it this way: "I like to move quick and people who lag behind really irritate me." I kind of hate to admit it, but I'm that way, too. But I tend to be so with a smile.

When I was in junior high, I took a class called home economics where students (mostly females) learned to cook and sew. Our first sewing project was a stuffed hippo. Why a stuffed hippo? I have no idea. Excited about the project, I purchased lime green terry cloth material and lace, for a mini hippo skirt. I had high hopes as I pressed my foot down on the sewing machine lever and started my first seam. The first few inches were great. And then I made my first mistake.

I remember walking up to the teacher with a mess of balled up thread. She introduced me to something called the seam ripper. For the non-sewing reader, a seam ripper is a little tool that rips out all the seams you just put in. It should really be called a backtracking device. Did I mention I hate delays? Well, I really hate backtracking delays. I like to move forward. *Forward!* I guess that's why I don't really like to sew.

———

There's a joke in our house that if we can't finish a project in one day, we won't do the project. One day, years ago, I was getting ready to have company for dinner. As I was cooking lasagna, I noticed that the kitchen could really use a coat of paint. One problem: I didn't have a lot of time. So, between noodles boiling and the meat sauce simmering,

I rummaged around in the garage. Before long, I found what I was after: white paint.

Due to time constraints, I tackled the job in the quickest way possible. I took nothing, absolutely nothing, off the walls. I painted around everything. I'd brush a few strokes, reach over and stirred the meat sauce, and then get back to my painting. I am embarrassed to say that I even painted around my wall calendar. Now that likely saved me two seconds!

In daily life, delays are irritating at best. They try our patience, cause us to be late and foul up our schedules. But the real test is how do we cope when God pulls a delay? When God delays answers. When God seems silent and far away.

It didn't take me long to discover that, unlike last-minute paint jobs, medical problems often mean delays. With medical problems things can move very slowly. My situation was no exception. I was about to experience some huge disappointments, loss and delays that would cause me to question God and His plan for me.

The day before I was scheduled to have my left breast removed, I wrote this in my journal: *"What does one do the night before they have a breast removed? I have never done this so I don't know how. Do I say good-bye to my breast? Do I take a picture of it, to remember it? Silly, I know. Please take care of me, Jesus."*

Monday, July 8. Four months into this journey, and I was about ready to have a mastectomy. I was tired. So tired. Brian and I got to the hospital and I went through the normal processing routine. I was in the pre-surgery area, hooked up to an IV, waiting for my plastic surgeon to speak to me. I had had some complications with my lumpectomy. That surgical site was still healing. My doctor explained to me earlier that if the site were not completely healed, he would not be able to perform the mastectomy.

Going into that day, I was concerned that my doctor would cancel the surgery. I asked Brian to hold my hand. I was so nervous and worried, I couldn't even pray for myself.

The surgeon came in, took one look at my surgical site and asked to talk to my general surgeon (the one who would be helping with the surgery). They stepped out of the room and I looked at my husband with tears in my eyes. "Do you think they are going to cancel it?"

We looked at each other and began to pray. As Brian prayed, my heart was screaming, *"Why, God? Why would you do this to me? Why have I come all this way, only to be hooked up to an IV? Don't you realize how hard this is? I don't want to prepare myself emotionally again for this. I don't want to have another 'last night' in my house with two breasts. It's too painful. Why do you always leave just when I need you the most? Where are you?"*

My surgeons stepped back into the room and broke the news. My surgery would be delayed. They couldn't tell me for how long. They said something about risk of infections …that this was for the best… To me, their words sounded like a Charlie Brown chorus, *blah de blah, de blah de blah.*

Delayed. I really, really hated that word. I hated even more the rippling effects that word had on my life. This was way bigger than a seam ripper. I needed rescuing from my darkness of despair. I needed a ray of hope.

CHAPTER

Six

ENOUGH LIGHT FOR THE NEXT STEP

Some might call it a "light bulb moment." Maybe even an epiphany. The only way I can describe it is the moment when the first ray of light came shining into my darkness.

The year was 1969. I remember one of the most exciting weeks of my whole sixth grade year was when we loaded up the bus, left the relatively safe confines of our school's playground, and headed off to the adventures of Science Camp. I became aware of Science Camp while in third grade. I talked about Science Camp through fourth grade. By the time I was in fifth grade, my bags were packed.

Unfortunately, with all the talk and excitement came the warning of the dreaded "Night Hike." The hike took place down a steep hill, in complete darkness. The number one rule of the Night Hike: No flashlights. No exceptions. That was the rule.

As a sheltered sixth-grader, I thought to myself, "That's silly, I'm sure they must give you some light. After all, how could they let us walk down the hill in the dark? We're not even teenagers!"

Soon after arriving at camp, a fellow student asked a counselor about the Night Hike. Sure enough, no flashlights. Yikes.

The night of the hike came quickly. Why, I thought, did this night seem so dark? Where was the moon? Where were the lights shining from distant cabins? That night, they were nowhere to be found.

And then it was my turn to walk down the steep hill. The rules were, you had to keep walking until you saw the light from the counselor's flashlight. As I stepped away from the familiar and from the voices of my friends, the darkness of the night seemed to wrap itself around me. I could see nothing. I remember putting my hand in front of my face. I couldn't see my hand. Nothing.

The walk seemed much longer than I am sure it really was. I remember the rush of safety, of security that I felt as soon as I saw the flashlight's beam. It was like the brightness of the light was shouting words of comfort and peace to me, breaking the power of the darkness with its double-C batteries. I knew when I had made it. I had completed the task. I had made it through the darkness. I was going to be fine.

It was a most significant day when the first ray of hope came shining into my breast cancer crisis. I had had a sad morning. I woke with a heaviness that I just could not shake. I was grieving the loss of my breast before I even lost it. I was incredibly, incredibly sad.

I remember going to the kitchen sink to rinse the highlighter out of my hair (hey, even in our deepest sorrow, a girl's gotta have good highlights!). As I let the water pour over my head, the tears and sobs poured forth. The noises that came from my sobbing were from that deep, deep place in my heart where pain resides.

And then I felt a familiar hand rubbing my back. Not saying a word, just letting me know that she was there. My oldest daughter, Allie. She just let me cry.

I finished rinsing my hair and I knew that the sink wasn't going to cut it. So, I moved to the shower. As soon as I stepped into the shower and felt the comfort of the warm water, the tear floodgates opened. As I let the water wash my tears down the drain, I cried out to God. I told Him how sad I was. How painful this journey was. How scared I was. I told God how I dreaded standing in front of my husband for the first time with only one breast.

And right there in the midst of all my pain, the Lord met me. It was as if there was no hiding from Him. I remember being bent over, sobbing, not even able to stand straight, tears streaming down. It was at that moment that God spoke to me. He said, "Pattie, can you trust me? Can you trust me that life can be even better than you've known it so far?"

There it was. The first ray of hope. I answered Him in a weak voice, "Okay, I'll trust you. I don't see it yet, but I'll trust you."

I stepped out of that shower with a renewed sense of hope and peace.

The crazy thing about living a life of faith and letting go of control is all the unknowns. Living a life of faith means you only get enough light for the next step. I have always been one who wants the whole path lit up before me so I can see exactly what's up ahead.

Still, like the counselor's flashlight, God's words came to me. The promise: Life could be better and brighter than I had ever known it could be.

CHAPTER

Seven

I WANT MY OLD LIFE BACK, BUT...

"Don't forget to say thank you, Pattie." These were words that flowed often from my mother's lips. Being a grateful person is something that I have had to learn. I didn't arrive on the planet with a thankful heart. I arrived with complete selfishness, wanting things —like Sinatra did—my way.

I have learned to be thankful when nice things are done for me. It's not that complicated really. Someone opens the door for me, I say, "Thank you." When offered dessert, I respond: "Yes, thank you." It's such an easy thing to say. Thank you. I have become an expert in the art of gratefulness. Here's the equation by which I live: Acts of kindness = a thankful response. Easy.

As I have grown in my relationship with Christ, I've become aware of scriptures challenging my equation. An example:

1 Thessalonians 5:18, "Give thanks in all circumstances for this is God's will for you in Christ Jesus."

Does this mean I must be grateful even in the middle of a crisis? How could God possibly expect me to be grateful for breast cancer?

I awoke one morning, two weeks before my surgery date, and went for a walk. As I walked I began to realize how angry I was. I was sick and tired of breast cancer. I was exhausted from grieving for the part of me I hadn't yet lost, and I was emotionally wrung out. As I walked it became clear to me that I was indeed mad at God.

Friends would ask me: "Have you gotten mad at God yet?"

"Not really," I'd reply rather meekly.

But on that day, two weeks before my surgery, the anger came.

I took my anger out on those around me. I was short-tempered with my husband and my children. I withdrew from friends. I got irritated when my parents or siblings would call to see how I was doing. I didn't want to talk to them. I punished them with my curt answers and cold voice. I was on staff at a church at the time and I found staff meetings unbearable. Everything and everyone irritated me.

Here's an excerpt from my journal, dated July 27, 2002, two days before my mastectomy: *"I'm finding that tackling the routine, mundane stuff in life is so very difficult. I catch myself getting angry about phone calls relating to work or anything else for that matter. I get angry for the disruption in my day. I had a strange experience a few days ago. I was at work and it was the day of our staff meeting. I was dreading it. It had been a rough morning and my emotions were right on the edge. I found it totally annoying to be planning two months out when all I could think of was my surgery in two days. Then came lunch. I sat around a circle of people that I knew cared deeply for me, but I found their conversation irritating, at best. Laughter was ear-piercing. All I wanted to do was cry. A friend told me later that I looked like I was standing on the outside of a party looking in. That's truly how I feel. Being so fragile is not fun. Sometimes I feel so out of control of my emotions I don't know what I'll do next."*

As I continued my walk, thoughts of anger filled my mind. Tears were now streaming down my face. I hate walking and crying, so in a lame attempt to create some privacy I pulled the hood of my sweatshirt over my head and started to pray. I prayed out loud in the quiet safety of my hooded cocoon.

I told God how mad I was, how long this journey had been already, and how much I hated having breast cancer. In the middle of my griping and complaining, God gently reminded me of a few things. He said: *"Pattie, every day along this journey I have sent you comfort and help in many different ways. Sometimes it was a simple phone call from an old friend. Your mailbox was stuffed full of cards from well-wishers and offerings of prayer. Friends and family members dropped off meals, oftentimes unexpectedly. Your sister and your girlfriend cleaned your house twice a week for weeks. On Friday (so it would be clean for the weekend) and again on Monday (because they understood that families make messes and they knew it would need some 'sprucing up.'). Flowers were dropped off on your front porch. Someone anonymously placed a banner on your garage door with the words, 'Jeremiah 29:11 We're Praying for You!' All of these were gifts from me.*

I just used people to carry out my plan. Oh, some days you recognized the gift was from me, but other days you were too resentful and mired in self-pity. You missed my presence."

God got my attention. As I walked along my heart began to change. It wasn't like some lightning bolt or blinding light from heaven, rather it was the quiet voice that caused by heart to change. It was as if the Creator took my fist of rebellion that was raised high in the sky and slowly released the tension in my fingers, and intertwined his fingers with mine. He took my heart of stone and with His tender touch brought life, miraculously, back into it. The Creator of the universe reached down and touched His creation.

My prayers began to change, too. Complaints changed to prayers of gratefulness. I told God how sorry I was. I began to thank Him for everything around me. I thanked Him for healthy legs to walk. I thanked Him for my lungs to breathe. I thanked Him for the birds, the trees and the grass. Then, I started for the first time to be thankful for the medical team that was treating me. Instead of being so mad and resentful that I had to have a plastic surgeon, I praised God that at least I had a good one. Without realizing it, I had begun to view the medical people in my life as the enemy, instead of the blessings they truly were.

I walked for two miles. When I rounded the corner and started for my front door, I was a new woman. From the inside out, I had been completely transformed.

On July 29, 2002, my left breast was removed. This has been the most difficult experience of my life. But God in His faithfulness never once left me alone. I would never have learned this if I didn't go through these trials.

It's been said that if you want to fish for pearls you've got to dive into deep waters. God called me into deep waters on July 29. And I can honestly say I am grateful for the things I have learned. True, I wished I did not have to lose my breast, but I would never want to go back to the way life was before I lost it. I am a better person now, because of this experience.

CHAPTER

Eight

SURVIVING VS. THRIVING

I awoke with a dry mouth, messy hair and a bandage that covered the left side of my chest where my breast had been. The bandage was padded with three inches of gauze, which gave me the false impression of being normal. The pain, however, was a strong reminder that I was anything but normal. Everything ached. I felt like I had hardly slept, and yet there were six unaccounted hours. I must have dozed off during the night.

Then, morning came. Ah, morning. Typically, morning is my favorite time of the day. If I were home, I would be making noise… the noise that is heard only at the start of a new day. The opening of blinds, the start of breakfast, feeding my dog, waking my kids. You know, the noises that confirm that joy really does come in the morning. I would have been standing on my front porch kissing Brian goodbye at about this time. I would have stood there and watched him get into his car and drive away to another day of work. But none of those comforting noises reached my ears on the fifth floor of Kaiser Hospital that day. That morning, what reached my ears was upsetting medical noises. The voices of doctors and nurses, carts being rolled down the aisles, breakfast trays being delivered. I wanted no part of this hospital-sounding morning.

I lied there, listening to the new morning noises, and sub-consciously place my hand on top of the bandages. I wanted to be brave and pull back the white gauze. I wanted to take a quick look. I was too scared. *Maybe when Brian gets here.*

My thoughts went to the events of the previous day. I remembered the last thing my doctor said to me before the anesthesia took effect. She spoke words of comfort. She would take care of me, she said. I was going to be fine. Fine. Such a simple word for such a complex situation.

I was relieved to see my husband, Brian, and daughter, Katie, walk into my hospital room. Their cheery smiles and soft hellos brought me instant comfort. I was no longer alone with the noise. Even though I had a roommate, the woman on the other side of the curtain brought me no company. The language barrier and my emotional state prevented us from engaging in conversation. There was more than a curtain separating us.

I told Brian and Katie that I wanted to look under my bandage, but that I was scared. Neither pressured me. No lectures on bravery. They just showed compassion and understanding. I laid there listening as they began chitchatting about their morning. Listening to their delicious, warm voices filling the cold room, I found myself slowly pulling the tape that protected me from my new reality. This was it. The moment of truth.

I was not brave enough to completely pull back the bandage, but what I did see surprised me. Due to my choice of starting my reconstruction the same day as my mastectomy, I had a slight bulge under my skin. I even had a little cleavage. I was happy about that. The cleavage was there with the help of an expander that my plastic surgeon had placed under my skin. This expander was the start of the reconstruction process. For the next eight weeks, I would go weekly to the doctor's office and get the expander filled with more saline. The reason for this process was to stretch the skin so it can receive the implant. This would require a further surgery.

Whew! I had peeked. That was the first step in a series of many difficult steps for me.

Later that morning my doctor came in and said, "Let's take a look."

Just hearing those words sent a wave of fear over me. It was time to see the whole thing. In one gentle pull of the tape, she exposed my greatest fear. From the moment I was diagnosed I was dreading this moment. Did I look as deformed as I thought I would? Yes, a little.

I did have some cleavage, but other than that I had a completely flat chest. A flat chest. The very thing every junior high girl dreams of growing past. The most difficult part was the missing nipple. Oh, how I missed my nipple. It was such an important part of my body and it made me feel feminine. It fed my babies and brought pleasure to my husband and me. Now, my nipple was gone, replaced by a three-inch scar.

———

I survived my hospital experience and now it was time to go home. Home has always been a refuge for me. It is a place to be myself. Be myself? Now? I wasn't sure who I was anymore. Not that my breast defined who I was, but who was I when I wasn't undergoing medical tests or grieving the loss of my breast? Would the old, carefree Pattie return? In the days and weeks ahead, I would learn not only to survive, but to thrive.

It was an awkward experience walking through the doors of my home. I did not feel instant relief. As I crossed the threshold I was keenly aware that I wasn't the same person that left two days ago. In two short days my life had changed. Not only was my body different, but I had changed emotionally as well.

I remember walking into my living room and sitting stiffly in a chair. I felt more like a guest than a family member. It felt like I was visiting some distant aunt who covered her furniture with thick, loud, sticky plastic. The kind of plastic that sticks to the backs of your legs, forcing you to sit very still. I found myself sitting very still, in my own home. Normally, I would walk in, kick off my shoes, shout to my family and get busy doing something. That day, I didn't know what to do. I just sat. It would take some time to feel comfortable in my home again, just as it would take time getting used to living inside my new body.

As the days passed, I became physically stronger. I was off my pain medications, and took short walks in my neighborhood. I tinkered around the kitchen and enjoyed doing little things for my family again. Physically I was anxious to resume my normal activities. My emotions, on the other hand, were still completely raw. I was teary most days and had trouble concentrating. I felt self-conscious. It felt as if the whole world was looking at my flat chest, like I had a sign around my neck that read, "Hey, did you know I don't have a left breast?" I know these thoughts were irrational, but they surfaced every day.

One low point in my recovery occurred a few days after I had arrived home from the hospital. I was in the bedroom and I had just undressed. I heard Brian's footsteps down the hall. I panicked. I ran over to my closet and threw open the doors looking for anything I could find to throw over me. By the time Brian reached our bedroom doors I was in a sobbing clump on the floor, my hands covering my face. For the first time in 24 years, I was embarrassed to be naked in front of my husband.

Brian reached down and gathered me up in his arms and let me sob. He said: "Pat, this is just a season in our lives, and we will get past this and some day we will be on the other side looking back." I held on tightly to him and to those words.

I decided then that if I was going to do more than merely survive breast cancer, the battle was going to be won or lost in my thoughts. My thoughts of shame, disgust, and insecurity. I had to deal with the feeling that I might never look good in my clothes again. I felt jealousy when I saw the covers of women's magazines, with all their bosomy galore. All of these thoughts would have to be fought, for me, with the truth of God's words. So, I took some colored paper and cut it out into the shape of daisies and hearts. On these cutout flowers I wrote down scripture that helped me focus on how much God loved me. Scriptures like:

"Though I walk in the midst of trouble you will revive me, you will stretch out your hand against the wrath of my enemies and your right hand will save me." From Psalms 138:7-8.

And: *"For I am the Lord your God who takes hold of your right hand and says to you, 'Do not fear; I will help you.'" From Isaiah 41:13.*

I put the hearts and daisies in a large circle on my bedroom mirror. I knew that looking in that mirror was going to be tough for me. These words and images would help gird me for my battles.

———

It was a monumental day when Brian and I got up at 3 a.m. to go to one of his favorite fishing spots. We were headed to beautiful Silver Lake, located 52 miles east of Jackson, down Highway 88. Silver Lake has always been a place of rest and relaxation for Brian. It is a place to unwind from the hectic lifestyle of San Jose and the Silicon Valley.

One of the wonderful things about Silver Lake is that it's only three hours from our home. We wanted to get there early enough to see the sunrise. It was two months past my surgery when we hiked in to the lake. We had a great day together and just reveled in the outdoors. The sky was that real bright blue that makes even Paul Newman's eyes look a tad gray. The temperature that day was about 55 degrees. The air had a bite to it as if it were coaching us to walk faster to keep warm. As we walked and took in the nature around us, I felt the stress roll off my shoulders. I was breathing deeper, and enjoying the smell of fresh pine trees. I love that kind of breathing.

When we arrived at our spot, I had a crazy thought. I told Brian that I wanted to jump into the lake. We hid behind a rock and in the outdoors and changed into our swimsuits. Then we stood on the edge of the lake. On the count of three we would jump.

As soon as I yelled, "Two!" I was jumping in with the loudest scream I could muster. I came up laughing and yelling for Brian to jump in, too. The water was freezing!

We didn't linger, but I was happy we'd made the leap. To me, it was a symbol that I was jumping back into life. Not just surviving, I was thriving.

CHAPTER
Nine
COLD NIPPLES AND WINDING ROADS

I had to laugh out loud when the doctor handed it to me. "You have got to be kidding," were the first words out of my mouth.

The plastic surgeon sensed my surprise and explained, "Many women use these if they don't have a nipple. You simply peel off the sticky back and place it where your nipple used to be."

With sarcasm in my voice, I replied: "Oh, of course, how silly of me to not think of that myself."

It never occurred to me that an EKG lead could be used as a nipple. The object has a clear, round plastic sticker with a metal snap in the middle of it. My surgeon handed me a few and encouraged me to give them a try.

As I stepped out of his office, I shoved them into my pocket. Several thoughts were running through my head. One of them: "Won't I always seem cold on that side?"

I had two months to wait until I could undergo my last and final surgery, nipple reconstruction. I had completed my expansion process and, thankfully, had no complications receiving my breast implant. I was on the final lap of my journey.

During my journey through grief and loss, I pondered the question: "When will I get past this chapter in my life called breast cancer?" I have come to the conclusion that it is never far behind me. You might say, instead of walking arm and arm with me, it's a few steps farther back. The experience of breast cancer is still a big part of who I am today. For that I am grateful. I am grateful because I don't ever want to forget the lessons that I have learned. I am quietly reminded of these lessons every time I see a commercial or advertisement about breast cancer, or I hear of another woman who has been diagnosed.

With these images my mind conjures snapshots of my own journey. It is as if I am sitting in my grandmother's attic and I'm opening a dusty trunk full of black and white photographs. Each photo has captured a moment in time. I view these images as my own personal souvenirs, my memories. As I pick up one particular photograph, it's as if the scene comes to life....

There is a long, windy road that's lined with beautiful trees heavy with autumn leaves. There I am walking down the center of the road. It is toward the end of the day when the shadows are beginning to lengthen. I am dressed in my bathrobe and slippers and my hair is pulled back in a messy ponytail. My hands are dug deep into my robe pockets. I am moving slowly, unlike my generally energetic self. The road in front of me is long. I am just starting off. Upon closer look, I can see that I am not alone. I have a partner. His arm is intertwined with mine and he is leaning in, whispering something into my ear. The words that are spoken bring a smile to my scared and frightened face. They are sweet, refreshing words that lighten my heavy feet. What power ... what compassion...what tenderness...Who is this partner? This soul mate? This friend of mine?

He says his name is Jesus.

As we walk closely, he leans over and tenderly with his first two fingers lifts my downcast chin. I do not resist. As I lift my hanging head, he points in the direction of the trees that are lining the path. I smile. Then he points to what's lined up under those trees. My eyes focus in, and I see that along the road are gathered familiar faces. Standing under the first tree is my husband, Brian, and our three children. Next to them are my parents and siblings. As I walk farther down the road, my eyes go from one side to the other and under each tree are friends and family, familiar faces that are smiling at me. There are some faces I haven't seen in years. I ask my partner, "What are they doing here?" He replies, "Take a closer look and you will understand why they have gathered here."

I do as he says. Suddenly, it becomes clear to me. Some have their heads bowed and they are praying for me. Others have their hands raised in victory and they are shouting and cheering me on. The rest are gathered along the edge of the road with tears streaming down their faces.

As I look around and take in the scene before me, my eyes, too, are filled with tears. With my shaky hand covering my quivering mouth, I speak these quiet words: "You sent them here for me." His eyes are so filled with love and compassion that no answer on his part is needed. I know why he has sent them. I felt my burden ease as I walked farther down the road.

Then, just as suddenly as the road had appeared, it took a sharp turn to the left. The smooth path to which I had become accustomed turned rocky and uneven. The autumn trees have disappeared, replaced by piercing thorn bushes. I hold tighter to my partner's arm. I slow down and ask him what is going on. "Where are all the beautiful trees? Where did all my loved ones go? Why is the path so unclear now?"

With a gentle arm around my shoulder, he says, "This is the part of the journey that's meant just for us. There are many lessons to be learned, character to be refined, and love to be shared between the two of us."

As we continue to walk, I find myself stumbling on the uneven path. Now both of my arms are tightly wrapped around his big strong arm. I ask if we can turn around and go back to the main road. "We must continue going forward," he says.

The next stretch of road has unexpected twists and turns and often the path is dark. I have to completely depend on the strength of the one by my side. I learn to trust his judgment and to rely on his wisdom. It is obvious to me that he is the expert and has traveled this road with others before me.

It is a significant moment when my Savior leans over and says, "We are coming to the end of the dark, uneven part of the journey and once again we will rejoin the smooth path."

I am excited, but at the same time I have a question, "Why did we have to leave the smooth path in the first place?"

He replied, "You needed to depend completely on me. You needed to find out that I was all you needed. I was more than enough."

With these words still ringing in my ears, the path turns slightly and the sun breaks through. The trees are once again lining the path and the familiar faces are there. The only thing in the picture that changed is me. I am no longer walking slowly wearing my bathrobe. I am dressed in my jogging suit and my chin is held high. I am walking quickly, with a determined look on my face. As I pass by, I hear someone from the crowd ask, "Where is she going?"

The answer comes from a familiar voice that had walked each step of the journey with me, "She's moving forward, embracing life."

CHAPTER

Ten

THE VIEW FROM MY REAR VIEW MIRROR

Life's blessings come in all kinds of packages, wrapped in all kinds of paper, delivered by all kinds of people. Often, these packages arrive unexpectedly. On a warm August morning, one week after my mastectomy, I received such a gift. It did not come with the traditional ribbon and bow. It was not accompanied by a greeting card. Rather, it came from the view in my rear view mirror.

I was sitting in the parking lot of a shop called "The Next Step." It is a store in which women can find mastectomy bras, prosthesis, undergarments, and other clothing items.

I had asked my friend, Sally, to come with me on that difficult day. Breasts, like shoes and mittens, generally come in pairs. I had never shopped for a one-breasted bra before. I knew I was going to need Sally's support, her humor, and her ability to sit in silence, if that's what I needed. I was teary most of the way over to "The Next Step." I asked Sally, "What if the salespeople aren't sensitive to my situation? What if I can't find something that will fit? What if this confirms that I really won't look good in my clothes?"

I saw the front of the store when we pulled into the parking spot. *A far cry from Victoria's Secret. No supermodels in the window, no sexy lingerie. No fun.* These were my thoughts. I looked at Sally and said, "I don't want to go in. I'm scared."

Sally, in her loving and determined way said, "How about I go in and check it out for you?"

I sighed with relief. "That would be great," I said.

As she jumped out of the car and shut the door, I was left alone with the quietness of the still car, the kind of quiet that calls for library voices. It was too quiet, and I was sweating. Trying to cover up my surgical drain and the gauze that covered my wound was no simple task. With no thought to the weather that morning I had worn a white blouse, jean skirt and a cute baby blue button-up sweater. The sweater was becoming less and less cute as my skin dampened.

My mind was conjuring up pictures of what Sally might be doing, what she was saying, what the store looked like on the inside. I was glancing up every few seconds to look back through the car's mirror to see if could see anything. This went on for 10 minutes.

Then, I glanced up and saw the craziest thing. There was my friend walking out of the store with half of a mannequin in the shape of a woman's body displaying a mastectomy bra. Sally came out of that store like she was in a marching band (and she was the one chosen to carry the school flag!). I was laughing so hysterically as I watched her open the car door and squeeze herself and her new friend into the front seat.

"Well, here's a sample of what they have," she said.

"You brought the entire display out to the car? Are you crazy?" I asked. We both laughed as she did her best to mimic the sales pitch she had heard inside. She showed me the pros and cons to this particular bra and also reassured me that the women inside the store were not the monsters I had feared. Not a sharp claw or fang among them.

Little did I know that the sight I would see in the rear view mirror that day was exactly what I needed. How refreshing it was to have some comic relief. And Sally was right, there were no claws and fangs, but I did find myself scared and skeptical as I entered the boutique. The two women immediately called me by my name, thanks to Sally who had gone in before me and shared with them my story.

Not wanting to reveal any more than necessary, I quietly assessed the saleswomen who were behind the desk speaking to me. I made a quick decision on who I wanted to help me, with no logical reason for my choice other than the woman's kind face. Her face reminded me of the first day of elementary school, and how kids are always hoping that their teacher is the cute, young-looking one with the kind face.

The woman escorted me back to the dressing area. She not only had a kind face, but she also had a soothing voice that went along with her sweet personality. She handed me a burgundy silk blouse to put on in place of my white blouse and cute, albeit slightly damp, blue sweater.

"Why do I have to put on this silly blouse?" I wondered. I soon realized it was to keep me covered up while I waited for her to bring in the various bras I would be trying on. As I let the burgundy blouse slip off my shoulder, I wondered what her reaction might be. How would she respond to my one-inch thick bandage that covered up my left side and a drain that was taped to my tummy? The drain was there to collect blood and fluid that came from my wound. What a strange word—*wound*. It almost sounds as if I were injured in battle. Perhaps that's the real truth. I had been injured in a battle for life.

The saleswoman didn't flinch, nor did she seem upset by my new landscape. She asked me questions about my surgery and recovery, all the while she quietly went about slipping my new bra over my shoulders. She had soft hands and smelled of White Shoulders perfume. She fussed over me like a mother caring for her new baby. She made sure I was comfortable and that the bra's fit was right. Ever so gently, and with no judgment, she showed me how the snaps worked and where to slip in the cotton material to create the *look* of a breast. I finally felt safe.

I walked out of the store that day with a pretty white boutique bag that held my new bra and extra cotton. The items had been carefully wrapped in white tissue paper with a sticker from the boutique, in case I ever needed to go back. What a daunting thought. I was relieved when this shopping trip was over.

Still, I wished so very badly that I was carrying a pink and white-striped bag with pink tissue and the words *Victoria's Secret* written on the side.

CHAPTER
Eleven
SWEDISH AFTERSHOCKS

I was only going to run in for a minute. I grabbed a grocery cart and quickly started up the first of just three aisles I would need to go down. Glancing at my list for reassurance of a list I already had in my head, I turned the corner heading for the produce aisle. As I swung my cart my eyes spotted a six-foot display of pink ribbons and pink crepe paper. I looked again for confirmation that what I thought I was seeing was indeed true. My second glance confirmed the first: October is *Breast Cancer Awareness Month.*

Under the hanging pink crepe paper was a table covered in a pink tablecloth. Sitting on the very pink table were caramel apples wrapped in cellophane, and tied with a pink ribbon. Standing behind the oh-so-pink table was a college-aged woman dressed in a Swedish costume. Why a Swedish costume? I have no idea.

The Swedish maiden was calling out to any shopper that would give her eye contact to come and support breast cancer research by purchasing a caramel apple. I cranked my shopping cart around and headed in the opposite direction.

My body and my brain screamed: *I must get out of here!* I skipped the rest of the items on my list and headed to the checkout stand. By the time I exited the store tears streamed down my face. I was completely caught off guard by my reaction. Why was I crying? Why did I want to avoid the table with the sweet-looking Swedish maiden? Why couldn't I just go and buy $10 worth of caramel apples to support constructive work against a disease I hate?

It's easy for one to get perspective after some time has passed. It wasn't until later that day that I discovered I was having an aftershock. An aftershock is an unexpected moment that happens when life has returned to some state of normal, when you come face-to-face with your crisis once again.

The pink crepe paper and grocery store caramel apples symbolized such a painful part of my life. To have that pain simplified to a statement: "Buy a caramel apple and beat breast cancer," was hurtful to me. After all, here I was walking down the aisle of my grocery store with a reconstructed breast, a breast that has no feeling in it, that is a daily reminder that something precious was taken away from me. To have the ugly green giant of breast cancer infiltrate my grocery store (my grocery store!) felt like an invasion of my privacy. Up until then, the grocery store was a guaranteed safe haven where I wouldn't have to deal with that ugly green giant.

Aftershocks are the rippling effects of grief. If you throw a rock into a quiet lake, the rock will make a splash. That's the initial crisis. Beyond that are many ripples that come as a result of the rock entering the water. It helps to know that aftershocks are a normal part of the healing process. You are not just being overly sensitive or emotional. Those aftershocks are real.

So to the dear reader of this book, if you are experiencing an aftershock, please be gentle with yourself. Let the tears come and give yourself permission to grieve.

As I write the pages of this chapter I am once again facing an aftershock. In one week I go for my yearly mammogram. Since my mastectomy, I've had one clear mammogram. This will be my second round. I am, once again, facing that big green giant of my past. I woke up two days ago with my heart beating rapidly, and with fear in my gut. After sitting up in bed I realized I was stressing out about my upcoming appointment. I lay back down and silently prayed that God would relieve my fears and give me His peace. I recognized this "stress" as an aftershock and handed it right back to the one who created me.

I've learned that aftershocks are real, but I don't have to handle them alone. Even when they're sporting a Swedish maid costume.

CHAPTER
Twelve
WHERE ARE MY ANTS?

Ants in my kitchen. This is supposed to be the sign that life has returned to "normal." The ants are a sign that my all-consuming thoughts of breast cancer have ceased and that, once again, I can take a deep breath and let the smaller, more trivial things in life take center stage.

But instead, I find it has been weeks since I've taken a deep breath. My days are filled with uncertain thoughts because the possibility that breast cancer has returned and reared its very large, ugly head. You see, as I write this final chapter, I am three days away from a biopsy on my right breast. A hard mass has been detected and we must find out what it is.

And so I wait. I wait for appointments. I wait for telephone calls. I wait for test results. I wait on God.

As I think back on my journey through breast cancer and the lessons I have learned, I find that my faith boils down to this simple truth: God can be trusted. No matter what my circumstances, I can put my complete trust in God. He has a plan.

Am I scared? You bet. Have I cried? A lot. Do I wish this weren't happening? Absolutely.

Once again I find myself on the rocky, twisting and winding, thorn-filled road. I am again stumbling over uneven terrain, wishing so badly to be on the even pavement. But I do know that it is on the dusty, dirty, unknown path that I have found my most intimate time with God. I will continue to put one foot in front of the other, trusting Him to guide my future steps.

I believe that my future is full of hope—the hope of ants in my kitchen.

———————

Pattie's Note: It is weeks later, and with a grateful heart I write this final line….I am happy to report that I am currently cancer-free.

Epilogue, April 2007

As I sit at my computer to pen the closing lines of this book I picture my husband's long sleeved, comfy orange shirt with the words "Life is Good" written across it. That truly describes my life. Good. The dark days of cancer really are behind me. Never forgotten, but definitely behind me. I am amazed that with time comes healing.

Last year on April 6, 2006, my oldest daughter Allie and her husband Mike, gave me the honor of a new title. Grandmother! AKA...Nana Pat. That's right, sweet little Dylan Michael came into the world and stole all of our hearts!

My son Kyle and his wife Ruth have just purchased their first home! My youngest daughter Katie is just weeks away from high school graduation and will be attending a local university in the fall. This July Brian and I will be celebrating our 29th wedding anniversary! You see, life is GOOD!

As I consider all of these blessings in my life I can't help but wander back in my mind to that moment in the shower when darkness was penetrating my every thought and breath. That moment when God gave me a promise that came with a question when He asked if I could trust Him... that life could be better than I've known it so far? I think back to that day and I'm so grateful that I replied YES, I would trust Him. God has proven over and over to me that He indeed keeps his promises. Life is GOOD, and better than I ever thought it could be. And for that I'm forever grateful.

Acknowledgments

To my sweet husband, Brian who's sense of humor and strong shoulders I've come to depend on. Your ability to find humor even in the midst of sadness is a true gift.

Allie, Kyle and Kate, I would never have chosen to take you on this difficult journey, but I'm so glad you were there. Thanks for bringing a little bit of normal into my life when I had lost my ability to smile.

Mom and Dad, what can I say! The foundation of faith you laid for me as a child carried me through my battle with breast cancer. Thank you.

To my one and only sister, Sandy. Your endless support and creative ways you found to cheer me up amazed me. Thanks for letting me just be.

To Mike, Jeanie, Rick, Carrie, and Jim knowing you were praying for me touched me profoundly.

To my Birthday Club, thanks for listening, and understanding when I had no words.

To the many pastors at Hillside Church, who stood by me at some of my darkest moments.

To my girlfriend Sally, who taught me that any emotion at any given moment was perfectly fine!

To the sweet women at The Next Step Boutique, for your tender touch ,on one of my hardest days. I am truly grateful.

And finally, to my dear friends Sally and Heather for being brave

enough to join me in this adventure! To God be the Glory!
   I love you both!

Pattie

San Jose, California
July 15, 2007

Heather's STORY

To my two
MOMS
who loved me unconditionally.
My mom, Julie Hammond, who showed me how to be a mom and
My mother-in-law, Sandy Cheney, who gave me courage and strength

CHAPTER

One

OH BABY, MY BABY

*W*hat can I say? I'm a typical blonde. You may think that being blonde automatically stereotypes a woman. I prefer to think that I am only, at times, "intellectually challenged." Let me give you an example. Years ago, before my husband Adam and I were engaged to be married, we went to Africa to visit his aunt and uncle who were missionaries in Kenya. On the way, we had a 12-hour layover in London. Naturally, we were excited to be able to try and see everything in this brief amount of time.

One of London's most recognized attractions, of course, is Tower Bridge. We were headed in that direction, and found a good view of the bridge for a picture from London Bridge. Adam climbed up on the ledge to take a picture. Once on the ledge, he told me he was out of film, and asked me if I would get him another roll. I opened his backpack, found the roll, and tried handing him the whole container. Instead, he asked me if I would take the film out of the container for him. When I opened the container, it was stuffed full of cotton.

The first thing I thought was, I didn't know that you needed to pack film containers with cotton when you fly. Does this prevent it from exploding on the plane? I wondered. As I removed the cotton, I asked Adam, "Did you put this cotton in here so that the film would not explode from the elevation on the plane?" While I am certain Adam was having trouble containing his laughter, he said nothing as I proceeded to take out the cotton. Halfway through the canister, I

115

realized that there was no film.

"There's no film in here. It's empty," I said as I nearly threw the canister off the side of the bridge. Fortunately, Adam responded quickly.

"Just keep looking," he said. Still totally clueless, I was nevertheless intrigued. And there, at the very bottom of the canister, was an engagement ring. Through tear-filled eyes I could see Adam down on one knee, proposing marriage.

Looking back on this experience, I now see that I missed a number of clues that would have enabled most people to realize they were about to be proposed to. I tell you this story, dear reader, to give you insight into my way of thinking. At 24, I am still usually the last one to get a joke. It takes me even longer to learn what God is trying to teach me.

My story in this book is a painful one to me. It really is amazing how quickly joy can turn to sorrow. My story is one of the highest of joys and of the lowest of losses. Yet, the sustaining arms of God saw me through it all.

Here's my story…

My sister is my best friend, and my husband and my sister's husband are also close friends. The four of us bought a duplex together, so we live right next door to each other in Northern California.

We share nearly everything, and routinely plan dinners together, strategizing the week's menus and on which side of the duplex we will dine each night. My sister delivered her baby girl about one week after I found out about my pregnancy. This made my pregnancy even more exciting for Adam and I. Not only was it now "our turn," but we looked forward to our children being so close in age.

When I found out that I was pregnant, my excitement about this baby was the foremost thing in my life. I was determined to have a positive attitude about everything. I did not want to stress over changes in my diet, my exercise regimen, or my nausea. I was determined to focus on all that is good. We were having a baby, and we were going to be parents! To me, that was enough excitement to outweigh any of the downsides to pregnancy.

Like most mothers, I had been reading a baby book in order to keep track of the size and development of our baby week after week. Adam and I had already chosen names, and even had selected bedding items, depending on the baby's gender. If the baby were a boy, he would be called "Jackson Taylor," with a fire engine-themed room. If God chose to give us a girl, then "Isabella Grace" would have a strawberry-themed room. Adam and I both had a feeling that our baby was a boy, but we didn't really care either way. We even celebrated Mother's Day, and I received several cards honoring me as a new mommy.

We had wanted a baby for more than a year so, like most parents, we were ecstatic about the future addition to our family. And then 12 weeks into my pregnancy, my world began to fall apart.

CHAPTER

Two

THEN OUR DOCTOR DROPPED THE BOMB

On May 13, 2003, two days after Mother's Day, we had our first prenatal appointment with a doctor whom we had never met. I was a little nervous about whether we would like our new doctor, but I was confident God would work it out and that my baby would be fine. After all, people have perfectly healthy babies every day. Why wouldn't I?

Our 9 a.m. appointment meant that I had to take the whole day off from my job as a preschool teacher. Adam, a paramedic and knowledgeable about all things medical, was not working that day, and so we went to the appointment together. As Adam was driving there, he asked me to pray that everything would go smoothly. I remember praying that we would like our doctor, and that our baby would be healthy.

The staff at the doctor's office did all the routine stuff—urine sample, blood pressure check, weight check. When I finally saw the doctor I was relieved to find that she seemed both competent and friendly. I relaxed when the time came to listen to our baby's heartbeat. My stress level increased some when she could not initially find the heartbeat, but she assured me that this was nothing to be alarmed about. They would simply use a more sensitive ultrasound machine.

Once the doctor brought the ultrasound machine into the room, I realized that this test would be done vaginally and I totally freaked out. Up until this point, I had only had one pap smear done—and even then I cried through the procedure. So, to me, doing a vaginal ultrasound seemed like a very big deal. The doctor's relaxed attitude, however, calmed my fears, and I rationalized that I would just have to get over my misgivings. After all, I was going to have a baby. When she found the heartbeat, my emotions steadied, and when we saw our baby's little face on the ultrasound screen, my heart melted. As I lay on the examination table, I thought to myself, "This is it. I am really going to be a mommy."

But my elation was shattered when Adam said, "Wow, our baby has a really big head."

There was a long pause as we studied our baby's image on the screen, observing what looked to be something protruding from her head. My first thought was that whatever it was would simply go away with time. Then our doctor dropped the bomb.

She said: "Your baby has a cyst on the back of the head, and I am not sure of the complete diagnosis. I am going to need to send you to a specialized gynecologist to get it checked out."

The first thing that crossed my mind was that a cyst should be a relatively minor problem. Lots of people have cysts. Cysts can be drained or removed. Then, worry set in. What if it is serious? I asked the doctor what this all meant, and if my baby would be okay. She said that she didn't know. It could just be something that they could drain once our baby was born. I was comfortable with that explanation, but I was worried about the possibilities of "it could just be…"

As Adam and I stepped outside the doctor's office, we began sobbing, right there in the parking lot, with everyone staring. We did not know the extent of what was wrong with our baby, but we did know that we did not have a perfectly normal child. We did not have normal.

As we drove away from the doctor's office, I had an ache in my heart to see my mom. Unfortunately, she was at work; so instead, I told Adam that we should go see his mom. Adam's mom, Sandy, works at our church, and I knew that being around people, and having them pray for us, was what we needed most.

"Does the baby have all his parts?" Sandy asked when I found her.

"Yes, but there is also a large cyst on the back of the head," I said as I began to sob.

Sandy hugged me tightly and we cried together. Then she said something that helped me get through my entire pregnancy. Sandy said, "It's going to be okay, we are all going to love this baby no matter what."

At the time I thought that meant that if the baby were born with birth defects, we would still love him or her. But in retrospect, I know that God gave Sandy those words to encourage me once we found out that our baby would not survive.

We found out on Thursday of that same week that our precious little baby was a girl, and we immediately named her Isabella Grace, as we had planned. The specialist diagnosed her condition Cystic Hygroma, which typically means about a one percent chance of survival. I remember being on the cold, hard gurney, wearing nothing but a hospital gown. There were 10 pairs of eyes fixed on me as I lay staring at the ultrasound screen and thinking, *"This can't be happening to me. I am supposed to be having this baby."*

That same day the doctor did an amniocentesis to determine the prognosis of the Cystic Hygroma. It could have been as minor as learning disabilities, or as major as severe retardation, where even if she did beat the one percent odds, Isabella would never walk, talk nor eat on her own. And she would likely live only three to four years.

Of course, I feared the worst. I wanted Isabella more than life itself, but I also wanted her to be normal. My biggest fear was that she would survive to full term and be severely disabled. In order to protect myself, I prepared to lose her right away. I felt as if that mindset would be the easiest way to cope with the situation. Then Adam and I could try to get pregnant again, and not that much time would have been lost.

Believing that our baby was unlikely to survive, the doctors told us that we had the option of terminating the pregnancy. I was adamant about not wanting to even think about that option. When we left the office that day, we were told that they would not have the amnio results for 10 to 14 days. Those days were the longest of any in my entire journey.

CHAPTER

Three
A MOTHER'S LOVE

My little girl that God gave to me
Has great pain; how I wish it were a scraped-up knee.
It was so easy when she was three.

But today's pain involves her own motherhood.
She wants to be a mother as I think she should.

She wants to hold her baby oh so tight.
Keep her from harm both day and night.

But today the doctors brought bad news.
According to him, Heather and Adam must choose
What to do with this bad news.

They can bring the crisis to an end,
Or decide it's not their place to bend.

To put their faith in God above
And to just plain trust in His great love.

My darling daughter, it's so hard to watch your pain,
To watch your tears fall down like rain.

Today I can only think of you.

I'll always love you no matter what you do.
The final choice is up to you.

My heart is heavy with the strain
Of watching your tears fall like rain.

Written By: Helen Maples

Before I found out the results of the amniocentesis, it seemed everyone around me wanted me to just give up. One Friday morning, which I now refer to as Black Friday, I was talking with my mom and she told me that she and Sandy, my mother-in-law, had some concerns with me carrying our baby to full term. Basically, they wanted me to know that if I needed to end the pregnancy, they would stand behind my decision to do so. When my mom first mentioned the idea of ending my pregnancy, I did not understand what she was saying. Then I did understand, and I became so confused. My mind was a blur of questions, like "No way can I do this, are you people crazy? What has happened to these women who I trust so much? Why are you encouraging me to consider termination? Don't you love this baby?"

I did not understand why my own mother would want me to give up my baby. I did not realize that because she loved me so much, she was allowing me to choose, without fear or judgment. She was giving me the freedom to decide what I thought would be best for me. At the time, I had not yet experienced the love that only a mother can have for her child. In the later months of my pregnancy I began to get a glimpse of that love, as it grew for my Isabella.

Still, so many questions swirled in my mind: "What if carrying this baby is a health risk to me? What if this baby survives to full term, and then dies?" I felt like these things would be too much for me to handle emotionally. Even though I, personally, have always believed that abortion is wrong, I began to feel like termination might be the easiest action to take. After all, I reasoned, this baby wasn't going to survive anyway. It's just that I am saving her, and me, a whole lot of pain. After mulling for a day, I was pretty positive I wanted to go through with the termination. I just needed to speak with Adam.

Before I talked with Adam, I sought counsel from a dear friend of mine. When I told Patty that I was thinking about terminating the pregnancy, she asked me, "What if you do terminate this pregnancy and then by some miracle God told you that you didn't need to because He was planning on taking her home to be with Him just a few minutes after you had taken her life? Would you feel badly for the rest of your life about your decision?"

"What does it matter if I end now what God will do later?" I replied.

"Yes, I suppose you could look at it that way, too," she said.

After I finished talking with her, I went home and told Adam what I thought was the best thing to do. I was confident, and even mentioned that both of our moms thought that this was the best course of action. I told Adam that God would understand if we could not handle this. He would not judge us because He knows how much we love this baby.

Adam just sat there, listening patiently, as I rationalized my plan. I thought for sure that he would at least think about what I said. But he didn't need to think. He told me there was no possible way we could do this. He said he felt like we would be putting God in a box, and that it wasn't up to us to decide when Isabella should die. It was up to God.

I immediately got angry. While it appeared I was angry with Adam, I was really angry with myself. I screamed at Adam, saying: "I am *not* a baby killer! This is not something I want to do. This is something I need to do. I don't think that I can do this, emotionally."

"I do not think you are a baby killer," Adam said. "I just think that God has given this gift to us, and we cannot reject her."

"Yeah, easy for you to say. You aren't the one carrying her," I yelled back. "What if I carry this baby to full term, and she lives for a week, and then dies? I really don't think I could handle that."

What Adam said after that gave me strength during the most difficult days ahead: "Even if Isabella does survive to full term, and she lives one whole week, I think it would be the best week of our lives."

That was all I needed. I was now in hysterics.

I felt so ashamed and angry for wanting to terminate Isabella's life. The next few days were fraught with confusion and pain. How was I to process this experience?

At first I was angry at myself, then I wanted to blame someone else, so I got angry at my mom and mother-in-law, for telling me that I should consider terminating Isabella's life. But then I got angry with God, for not giving me a perfectly normal, perfectly healthy baby, like everyone else.

"How could you do this to me?" I screamed at God. "I just

wanted a baby, and now I am going to have to carry this baby, knowing that she will not live." I thought about the year in which Adam and I had tried to get pregnant, and I began to think that if we hadn't tried so hard to get pregnant, none of this would be happening. I couldn't believe that God would put me in a situation where I would even think about compromising my beliefs.

Still, when I read the word "terminate" in the same sentence as "Isabella," it saddens me to think I had been so willing to give her up. I think what hit me the most is that Adam referred to her by name, whereas I thought of her as just another baby. Hearing Adam call her "Isabella," the name we had chosen for the baby we had prayed for, helped me to place a higher value on her life.

Looking back, I can see that God was testing me and Adam, and even my mom and Sandy. He wanted to see if we really believed what we said we believed. Once I realized that terminating Isabella was the wrong choice for us, my strength and hope in the Lord were made even stronger. My character had been refined. Even though I was still confused as to what God was doing in my life, I began to realize that carrying Isabella was a special gift.

I had been chosen to be Isabella's mom, and I was inspired to be the best mom I could be while I had the chance. This does not mean that there were not days that I was angry. I still wished that I would wake up one day, and it would all be a dream. I so wanted her to be normal.

CHAPTER

Four

GOD, I'LL MAKE YOU A DEAL

It wasn't until 14 weeks into my pregnancy that we received the results of our amniocentesis. That test revealed that our daughter had Turner's Syndrome. During the waiting period for the test results, Adam and I had researched the various potential problems that our doctor said were strong possibilities—Trisomy 13, Trisomy 18, Downs, and Turner's Syndrome. I had come to the conclusion that Turner's was the least devastating to my baby, and offered her the best opportunity for as near to normal life as I could expect. So when the test results showed that Isabella had Turner's, I knew that God answered my prayer.

Turner's meant that Isabella would suffer no retardations. The biggest difficulties in her life would be a very short stature, a thickset, webbed neck, and the absence of ovaries. Adam and I both felt that these would be quite mild difficulties compared with the other complications the doctor had now eliminated. We began to allow ourselves to develop a strong love for her because we felt that she would be able to lead a relatively normal life.

As the weeks droned on, I began to experience all the things that at one time I had looked forward to, but now feared. I felt Isabella kick. I visualized what her face would look like, and I was building that special bond that only a mother can have with a baby that she alone carries within her body.

I had moved beyond falling in love with wanting a baby. I had fallen in love with my baby, Isabella Grace. Even though I knew it was

127

silly, I began to make a deal with God. I told God that He did not ever have to give me another baby, if He would just let me have Isabella. I believed that I wanted her more than most mommies who are having perfectly normal babies because I had been told numerous times that death would inevitably take her from me. People tried to tell me that because she was imperfect it would be easier if God would just "take her home."

I wanted to scream at people who told me that something was "wrong" with my precious little girl. My heart would cry out: "Nothing is wrong with her in God's eyes, and I know that if God chooses to bless me with her, I would always look at her as God does."

As Isabella grew, so did the cysts in her body. The doctors were confident that it would be only a matter of time before her heart stopped beating. But God created Isabella to be a fighter, and her body grew. This meant that I needed new clothes. Maternity clothes. Something that was supposed to have been exciting turned into a tortuous event.

When I went to maternity shops, I was surrounded by pregnant women. Normal pregnant women. Normal pregnant women who were excited about their bodies and babies. As if this weren't bad enough, when I went to purchase a blouse, I had to answer a list of questions: Address? Phone number? Due date? Would I be breast feeding?

While I simply smiled and answered each question, my heart sunk. I wanted to scream, "My due date is irrelevant because my baby is going to die! Would you still like to know if I am planning to breast feed?"

After spending several hours walking aimlessly about the mall, I came home and sobbed myself to sleep.

Fortunately, my mom came to the rescue. She took me to San Francisco for the day, helped me pick out some new clothes, and we turned a difficult day into an enjoyable and meaningful time —something moms are especially good at doing. Once again, my own mom was modeling to me what being a mother is all about.

CHAPTER

Five

TRUST AND SURRENDER

The doctors told me that once Isabella died, the easiest procedure would be a dilation and extraction, commonly referred to as a D & E. I was uncomfortable with a D & E for several reasons. First, in the state of California, a doctor could only perform this procedure up until 24 weeks. Second, I wanted to be able to see Isabella and hold her, like every new mommy. The doctors told me that this would not be possible after a D & E. Third, I discovered if I chose this procedure I would be put under anesthesia and Adam would not be permitted into the operating room with me.

I pictured myself being wheeled away from Adam as I went to have our baby taken out, never to see her. In my heart I knew that I would need to be able to envision Isabella in days, weeks, months, and even years to come. From this moment on, I determined that I needed to do everything that I could to validate her life, and give it meaning. I began yearning to do things that every new mom would do. I wanted to feel like I had enjoyed the precious little time God had given me to spend with her. This is when I first believed that God really was going to get me through to the other side, because He helped me to realize how much I needed to deliver Isabella, just like any other baby.

On June 21, 2003, I had Isabella dedicated. My niece was dedicated (in a ceremony much like a baptism) on Mother's Day, and I wanted to acknowledge that Isabella, too, was handcrafted by the Lord, even if she would not survive to full-term. When I first decided to have Isabella dedicated I felt a bit embarrassed to ask people to attend this service. We had already joined together to pray for Isabella. I felt like people would be wondering why I wanted to repeat what had already been done.

Fortunately, people did not think that at all. In fact, everyone thought the dedication was a great idea. My parents opened their home for the dedication, and were thankful that we would be doing something special to honor Isabella's life. My parents would be leaving the next week for three weeks in Europe, and both my mom and I had a feeling that Isabella might die while they were away.

My dear friend (and co-author) Pattie, who is also Adam's aunt, gave me words of encouragement, and even sent me home with some tangible memories. The dedication was a memorable time, especially for me as I now have verses, pictures, and other symbolic items to help me remember Isabella's life. I also wrote and read a letter to Isabella. I simply wanted to tell her how much we love her, and how much joy she brought into our lives, even for a short while. Silly as it might seem, I wanted her to know that we really did want her, not only when we thought she was healthy, but even when we knew she would be born with differences.

June 21, 2003

My dear, sweet Isabella Grace,

I am writing to let you know how much I love you and cherish every day I have with you. Your family has gathered around you tonight because we know that you are a gift from the Lord. I want to give you back to Him so that He is able to do His good and perfect will for your life, whether that be taking you home, or healing your body. I know that this journey He has put me on is not meant to be traveled alone. I believe that by giving you back to Him, I will be opening myself up to whatever the Lord chooses to do. I know that only He knows what is best for your life, and He doesn't want to put any of us through more pain than we can handle. I want you to understand that because we are giving you away, it doesn't mean we love you less, but rather we love you more. We wanted you before we even knew you were in my tummy.

Also, I don't want you to think that when we discovered you have Turner's Syndrome, that we just gave up on you. If anything, the opposite was true. I have wanted you even more after finding out that it was only Turner's. I believe that I am capable and ready to be blessed with a precious little girl who has learning disabilities, and differences, some of which I am probably not even aware of yet. Sometimes I am amazed at how much I love you when I don't even yet know you. I have only a vague image of what you look like... your smile and your tiny hands. I will never forget going to the doctor, after we already knew that you had Turner's, and being so amazed at watching your tiny little hand open and close. I like to imagine that you were waving at us in that ultrasound picture.

Even though you have only been a part of me for a short time, I feel as though a piece of my heart will go with you if God chooses to take you home to be with Him. Even though I want you more than words can describe, only God knows how much longer you will be with us. But that is okay with me. I am prepared for that because recently I have come to the realization that none of us knows how long we will be on this earth. So I have decided that from here on out, I am not going to mourn for something that has not even happened. Instead, I am going to celebrate your life, no matter how much time God gives me with you. Who knows? We could be together for a very long time.

I know it might seem a little scary at times, your tiny little body has suffered so many changes just in the past month. To be honest, I am scared, too. Every day it seems like I am faced with more decisions that I need to be thinking about, and prepared for, so that I can value your life as much as anyone's. I think the thing that scares me the most is any pain that you might be in now, or possibly have yet to come, as your little heart begins to fail. But I am constantly reminded that God will take care of you. I want you to know that you don't have to hold on to life for me or anyone else. Don't get me wrong, I want you, but I also want you to be free of pain, and when you do want to let go of fighting, you will be going to a much better place. It may not seem like it right now, but you are one of the privileged. There is one verse that your Grandma gave me that I want to share with you. It is Psalms 121:

I lift up my eyes to the hills, where does my help come from? My help comes from the Lord, the maker of Heaven and Earth. He will not let your foot slip. He who watches over you will not slumber. Indeed, He who watches over (Isabella) will neither slumber nor sleep. The Lord watches over you. The Lord is your shade at your right hand. The sun will not harm you by day or the moon by night. The Lord will keep you from all harm. He will watch over your life. The Lord will watch over your coming and going both now and forevermore.

Isabella, I want to claim this verse as your "life verse." Every time I read this verse I know I will think of you, and I imagine that if you go to heaven before I do, you will think of me when you read it also.

Sometimes when I am lying in bed at night, I try to imagine what you will look like…your smile, your eyes, the color of your hair. It's hard for me to picture you as a tiny baby, so instead I think of you as a toddler, with big blue eyes, light blond hair, and your mommy's nose. When I think of you, I don't see anything different about you. I see your neck as being beautifully perfect, without faults. I see you as being the smartest in school, without disabilities. I guess that's a mother's love. But I know that not everyone will see you as I do. If God does choose to bless me with you, I want to prepare you for this in advance. We live in a cruel and harsh world, and there may be times that you get teased or laughed at for your differences. But that doesn't mean that your family and true friends will love you any less. We love you because of your beautiful heart, not because you don't look like everyone else. The biggest comfort I have — if I am not able to keep you for myself — is knowing that you will be very well taken care of in heaven.

I am eagerly awaiting the day that I will get to see you and talk to you and get to know you. But, we do not know what the future holds, so until then, I will keep imagining what you are like and loving my dear, sweet Isabella Grace.

After the dedication services, I felt a renewed sense of hope, not necessarily for Isabella's life. Rather, I felt hope that God would see me through this, and make me a stronger person because of it.

CHAPTER

Six

I WANT MY MOMMY

The long days of not knowing if and when Isabella would die stretched out into weeks, and finally I found myself four and a half months pregnant. Eighteen weeks. I felt Isabella's movements more and more frequently. My tears fell more and more often. And the reality set in for how much love I had for my baby girl.

Each Tuesday we had our weekly visit to the doctor to find out if Isabella was still alive. Each Tuesday. Every Tuesday. One Tuesday I walked out of the doctor's office feeling fairly excited. Even though I knew that Isabella would likely not survive, the doctor mentioned, rather precariously, "There's always a chance that she *could* survive." That was all I needed to hear. I began to believe that God would indeed give her a chance. I was even telling people, "The doctor said she has a chance. You just never know. Maybe we will have a baby!"

The very next Tuesday, however, we went to the doctor and Isabella was not doing well. When the doctor performed the ultrasound, he noticed fluid around her heart, in addition to fluid in her liver, lungs, and abdomen. The doctor said that the fluid was probably causing strain to her heart, and it looked like she was going into heart failure. I came out of this appointment crying hysterically. Every emotion poured out at once—anger, resentment, fear, and sadness.

"I want her so bad!" I screamed at Adam. Adam just held me and comforted me, as we cried together on our couch. As we sat there, I realized how much I ached for my own mother's love. My parents were on vacation in Europe, and they would not be home for two more

133

weeks. It seemed as if they had been gone for so long. I began to realize that if Isabella died by the time our appointment came around the next Tuesday, they would miss seeing her by just one week.

"Isabella cannot die yet; surely God knows that I cannot survive if she dies before they come home. I want them to be able to see my little girl," I told Adam. I screamed to God, "Please, don't take her. I need my parents. I cannot go into labor without my mom and dad!"

The next Tuesday morning, before the appointment, I called my parents. I started crying because I was so scared that God was going to take Isabella before they returned home. My mom said that she was scared, too.

I went to the appointment with Adam and his mother Sandy, positive that God had not yet taken Isabella. I even thought I had felt her kick on the way to the hospital. As the doctor began the ultrasound, I searched for that tiny little heartbeat. In weeks past, I had been able to locate that oh-so-fragile *blip blip*. This day was different. Although it felt like hours, it must have only been a minute or two before the doctor said, "I just want you to know that I have not yet located a heartbeat."

I think I knew that Isabella was already gone, but I continued to fix my eyes on the monitor for at least another four or five minutes. I was sure that there must be a heartbeat in there somewhere, and that if I just kept looking, I would find it. I remember lying on the exam table, my stomach fully exposed, the machine still on, and the tears streaming down my cheeks.

Her heartbeat was never found again.

I can't even remember what happened next, but somehow I told Adam to get Sandy, who was in the waiting room. Sandy came in, and we sobbed and held each other close. Finally, I said, "What am I going to do? My mom isn't even home yet. I don't know what I am going to do. I don't think that I can do this without my mom."

Sandy just pulled me close and said, "I know, I know. But we are going to get through this, it's going to be okay."

Once I gained control of myself, the doctor asked if I wanted to induce labor that very day. I said: "No, can we wait until tomorrow? I need time to process all of this." This was my excuse for wanting to wait, but the real reason was that I secretly hoped that once my parents found out that Isabella had died, they would catch the next flight home. I knew that the only way they could get home in time was if I delayed being induced.

When I called my parents, they cried along with me. I was relieved that I was at least able to talk with them, but at the same time felt I needed them even more. Still, when I got off the phone, I was comforted with the thought that I had many people surrounding me who loved me…my grandmother, my sister, Adam's mom, and others who gave emotional and prayer support.

As the day slowly passed reality's full weight set in. I realized how much I missed my mom. I ached for her. I went to bed hoping and praying that she was getting on a plane, and that I would see her the next day. When the next day dawned, I called my parents. In Europe. My mom was still there.

Later that morning, I realized my mom would never see my baby. I was hysterical. I got angry at God, screaming, "Don't you realize how much I need her?" My sister walked into the room and I said, "Can't you call mom and tell her that I need her? Can't you tell her how much I want her to be able to see my baby? My baby is not coming home from the hospital. She won't get to see her, hold her and spend time with her if she doesn't come home right now."

My sister called her. But my mom would not be able to come home. Later, I found that there were no flights to get my mom home fast enough.

As I look back on this experience, I am reminded of the anger that filled me when God took my baby "too soon." Even though I will never fully understand why this happened, I am able to find some good in the experience. My mother-in-law and I were drawn closer together. Also, my sister was able to be for me what I needed from my mom during the delivery. I cherish that.

CHAPTER

Seven

THE HARDEST DAYS

During my pregnancy, Tuesdays were the hardest days. Every Tuesday we anxiously went to the doctor so that he could check on Isabella. God gave me the wonderful—and cursed—gift of optimism. Each time my husband and I went to the doctor, I was excited to see my baby girl, hoping that God was going to perform a miracle. I whispered to God: "Right now would be the perfect time to amaze this doctor."

Yet every week, every Tuesday, her body was slowly shutting down and I felt like my heart was breaking all over again. I wondered why God had put me through the pain of not knowing if and when Isabella would die. At times, I thought that it would be so much easier if He could have just taken her from me early. But once I gave birth, I realized why God allowed me to endure this pain.

My labor was induced on July 9. This was the most excruciating pain I had ever experienced. The doctors thought that the best procedure would be to insert laminaria, or wooden-like rods into my cervix. The first time, they inserted six rods. The second time, they took the first six out then inserted eight more into my cervix. When the rods were inserted, they were small, almost like a piece of tanbark (except skinny, about one inch long) covered in seaweed-type material. As these rods remained inside my body, they expanded to about three or four times their original size. This was in the hopes of opening my cervix to at least seven or eight centimeters. Because this was an outpatient procedure, I was given no pain medication.

On July 10, I was admitted into labor and delivery. When they extracted the second set of rods, I was dilated only two centimeters. Two. I still had at least five centimeters to go.

The hardest part of that day, despite the pain, was being surrounded by women in the ward who were delivering healthy babies. Although I was in a private room, I could hear heart monitors and the first cries of the newborn. This torturous experience was worth it once I delivered Isabella.

Holding Isabella in my arms and spending those cherished moments with her were worth the heartache. This was the first time that I was truly grateful for the precious little life that God had given me. After we went home from the hospital, Adam's mom, Sandy, said: "This was one of the hardest days of my life, but I would not have missed it for anything in the world." Sandy was with me when I delivered Isabella. She articulated exactly what I was thinking.

As I look back on my journey, I am amazed at what I have, and continue to, learn. I heard a familiar quote recently that reminded me of how wonderful Isabella's presence was in my life. The quote is from Tennyson: "'Tis better to have loved and lost than to never have loved at all."

I believe that Isabella was never meant to live on this earth. Rather, she was created and lived for a time so that my Creator could enjoy her, and He chose me so that I could learn to walk with grace, and to discover the true meaning of surrender.

I feel a great sense of honor that God chose me to be Isabella's mom.

CHAPTER

Eight

SURVIVING THANKSGIVING

I am a people pleaser. I have a selfish desire to want everyone around me to like me, and to be happy. I do not like to be angry and I do not like to be sad. I am also easily swayed by others' emotions. Bottom line: I am willing to do almost anything to make others happy.

Ever since I was a child people have described me as spirited, animated, and dramatic. I am an emotional woman. I can cry watching a television show, and 10 minutes later be laughing hysterically at a friend's joke. No one knows where this emotionalism comes from, because both of my parents, my sister, and my brother are all levelheaded, rather stoic individuals. For nearly half of my pregnancy, and even months after, I lost my exuberant spirit.

After I delivered Isabella, I didn't think my lack of life and energy could worsen, but it did. I was angry and hurting. I hated these feelings, but couldn't shake them. I felt as though I were sinking in a sand pit. I did everything I could to make myself feel better, including trying to convince others that I was dealing "just fine" with my pain. I went shopping, and tried to suppress my anger with new clothes. I tried to become more involved in the high school youth group at the church I attend, but some of the other volunteers had new babies. Very emotional for me. I began working again as a preschool teacher, trying to forget for a few hours a day that my life was falling apart. In addition to working full time, I enrolled in university studies. Full time.

I wanted to be busy for at least 12 hours each day, so that I would not think about what I really wanted to be doing this fall: planning for a baby. I felt that if I stopped even for a moment, I would sink back down into that sandpit. What I didn't realize at the time was that if you just survive the pain, you're probably not dealing with the pain.

When I was in the hospital, the doctors told us that we should abstain from sex for about six weeks after Isabella's birth. They advised us to not even try to get pregnant again, for at least three to six months. I understood waiting six weeks to have sex, but if these people thought I would not at least try to get pregnant right away, they were woefully mistaken. They were crazy.

Even though I love and miss Isabella, I also really wanted a baby. I figured if I could get pregnant again, and have a baby right away, then this would help me move on with my life. I believed that I just needed to have the hope of another child. Once Adam and I began making love again, I was a total mess. I would cry, wondering why I wanted another baby when all I really wanted was Isabella. I felt like I didn't even care about her life. I had two completely opposite emotions: I wanted to be able to have my own baby to hold, care for and love, but I also wanted to give Isabella's life the respect it deserved.

One sleepless and angry night, I began to journal:

I'm mad! I do not understand why, but there it is, all the time. Anger. Maybe it's because my sister's almost seven-month-old recognized me for the first time tonight. When I walked into their house, she crawled clear across the room to me, smiling and giggling the whole way. I want a baby so bad. Adam thinks I am just sad, but he doesn't know the rage and resentment that I'm holding inside. I have so many questions. Why did this have to happen to me? I wanted Isabella even though she had Turner's. Why didn't God let me have her? What is so wrong with me that God took her away? Why do I have to suffer with so much pain? Why can't I just get pregnant? When I do get pregnant, how will I ever be able to love that baby as much as I loved Isabella? What if I can't love the next baby as much? What if it hurts too much to love again? What if I don't, or can't, love another child? Please, God, help me! I'm so lost, so confused, so angry, so sad, so prideful to think that I deserve to have her, so selfish, so hurt, so devastated, so tired of wanting what I can't have back.

The more fears I seemed to have, the more task-oriented I became. I seemed to have forgotten that sex is also the selfless act of pleasing your spouse. Instead of talking about this with Adam, I went through the motions. I became a sort of machine. I knew exactly what to say and what to do to make Adam happy, without actually feeling any happiness myself.

Life just got worse when school began. I was so caught up in work, homework, housework, busy work, that I completely forgot Adam. I really thought we could save so much more time in our busy schedules if we only had sex when I was fertile. Think of the time we would save! In my irrational thinking, we only needed sex to create another baby. Obviously, this mindset began to damage our marriage.

Adam and I had grown very close when we were in the midst of crisis. But once the crisis ended, we were left to carry on with our daily lives. In addition to "dealing with my grief," I had taken on too many responsibilities with work, school, and youth ministry. I left little, or no, room for Adam and me. When Adam and I finally talked, I realized that I viewed sex as making a baby, instead of making love. I had focused on being busy enough to not be sad all the time. I was so busy that I failed to even think about Adam or his needs.

I slowly began to understand that it was okay to give myself some time each day to vent the sadness and to cry. Surprisingly, once I was able to grieve, I was able to be more loving and attentive. In order to give myself this time, I did have to cut back on my responsibilities. I had thought that the less time I left myself to think about Isabella, the more I would be able to move on with my life and to find closure. Boy, was I wrong.

The biggest mistake I made: Thinking I needed to be pregnant by Thanksgiving if I even remotely wanted to enjoy the holidays. I figured that if I were pregnant by the time Isabella was supposed to be born, on November 25th, then I would have a sense of hope for the future. I told everybody I wanted to be pregnant by Thanksgiving, or at least by Christmas.

I hadn't even thought that I might be setting myself up for disappointment. Getting pregnant by any given date was a lot of pressure, my friend Sally told me. "Thanksgiving is going to be hard no matter what," she said. "Being pregnant isn't going to make the pain go away."

While hearing this was difficult, I agreed that it was God who would choose when I would become pregnant again. I tried to smile.

By the time I got home I was really irritated. "What right did anyone have to tell me what I could hope for in life?" I said out loud. True, I could be faced with disappointment come Thanksgiving, but I would just have to deal with that if and when that time came. Even though that conversation angered and annoyed me, I told no one.

Instead, I wrote in my journal:

It is now November 6, and I just found out that I am not pregnant. No plus sign. No pink, blue or blinking sign of life inside. I am so angry that I have to wait another cycle to try to get pregnant. I feel like I am on this endless journey, and the end, having a baby, seems so very far away. I had hoped that I would be able to surprise everyone with good news on Thanksgiving Day. I wanted to be able to give everyone a little piece of joy in the midst of my sorrow.

I guess you know best, God. Actually, when I stop and think about it, a small part of me is relieved that I am not pregnant. Why would I want to even think of getting pregnant before Isabella's due date? Wouldn't that mean I didn't love her as much? I know it's silly, but I have this image of her looking down on me from heaven, and if I had gotten pregnant, wondering how I could move on with my life so quickly when I claimed to love her so much.

I eventually realized that getting pregnant by Thanksgiving was not the most realistic nor most important thing in the world. My plan was not God's plan, and I was silly to think I could ever have a better idea. For the first time, I understood that I could not bring Isabella back by having another baby. Although I still feel like I am sinking at times, I feel like I am more than just surviving. But I'm not yet thriving.

CHAPTER

Nine

WHAT IS THIS THING CALLED CLOSURE?

One Sunday at church, my dad, who plays the piano, dedicated a song to Isabella. The song was "Amazing Grace" and behind the congregation's words on the church's big screen were beautiful, scenic pictures of God's majesty. The last picture slide was one of Jesus in the clouds, holding a baby in his arms.

While most Sundays after giving birth to Isabella were difficult, this particular Sunday was traumatic. In a sense, my father's playing served as a eulogy, as we never had an official memorial service after Isabella's death. I was emotional during the service, and afterward my mother-in-law found me with my eyes swollen and red, and asked me how I was doing. Through sobs, I told her that I was okay. It was really that some days were just so much harder than others.

"Well, maybe now you will be able to find closure," she said.

Closure? Even as she said these words it began to sting. I wondered if she wanted me to move on so somehow she could feel better. Isabella had not even been gone for one month. I recall thinking that I would move on if I weren't such an emotional train wreck. That afternoon, I found comfort in my journal:

Closure? What is this thing called closure? People say that when tragedy strikes you need to 'move on with your life,' you should find this thing called closure. How do I go about moving on? And would someone please tell me where I can find this elusive closure? I am the type of person who likes to follow a set of directions. I read the instructions inside the box. I can follow instructions. Maybe there are

12 steps that I could follow to closure. Yeah, a 12-step plan!

On the other hand, what does it really mean to have closure? It is not as though I stay in bed all day. I'm not just sitting back waiting for the ache in my soul to magically disappear. I want to move past these feelings. I want to feel normal, but how? Am I expected to just forget that I was supposed to have a baby at home with me now? And what if I don't want to move on? What if I enjoy thinking about Isabella, even if that does cause pain? Somehow, my dreams make me feel closer to her. Besides, if I move on, am I saying to the world that I didn't care about Isabella, and want to replace her with another baby? At the same time, I do want to move on and have another baby. God, please help me. I cannot go through this alone. I feel like I am split in half. Maybe finding closure just means that I have accepted what God is doing with my life.

I used to think that finding closure was vital to becoming emotionally stable after loss. I have found a different perspective now. The word closure means to close or to put to an end. I knew from the start of my grieving process that I could not simply close the chapter, the box in my life marked "Isabella." In my mind, closure meant boxing everything up, and trying to forget. But, I also thought that if I ever wanted God to bless me with another child, then I would need to somehow move past the heartache.

One thing that has helped me feel closer to Isabella, and to grieve more easily, is her baby blanket. It is a one-foot square piece of soft pink fleecy material, edged with lace, and embroidered in one corner is "Isabella Grace." When she was born, the doctors bundled her inside this blanket so that I could hold her. Having something sentimental to hold onto, to cry with, and even to sleep with has made me feel like I am closer to her. I can almost imagine holding her again, and telling her how much I love her.

One day, five months after her death, I realized I had not slept with Isabella's blanket for several nights. I decided I was probably reaching the beginning of closure. I put the blanket away, and was excited that I no longer had the nagging ache inside me. This phase lasted about one week.

Then I fell apart. Pregnant women and babies seemed to be popping up everywhere I went. Also, after a visit with my grandmother, I realized for the first time that the best part of my week was spending time with my 11-month-old niece, Kayleigh. To top it all off, I went to a doctor whom I had never met, and with my medical chart in her hand, she asked me how my baby was doing.

I was shocked. While I've never actually read a medical chart, I'm pretty sure it says in there whether or not someone has recently had a stillbirth. I would think a doctor might glance at a patient's chart before walking into the room.

I was speechless. If she had taken just two seconds to actually look at my chart this could have been avoided. I stuttered and tried not to cry, then said, "Oh, uh, I lost my baby."

She did not seem to understand my words. "What? You lost your baby?" She said it as though she believed I had set my baby down in the shopping mall, and forgot to pick her up again.

"Yes, my baby had Turner's Syndrome, and she died at 20 weeks," I said.

She put her foot in her mouth again. "Oh, you mean you had a spontaneous abortion. Well, it is probably for the best, since she was not completely normal."

I wanted to scream back at her: "Normal?! What, exactly is normal? Is it being perfect? Because the last time I checked, none of us is perfect."

Fighting back tears, I nodded at the doctor and fled the room. When I reached my little white Neon, my body was shaking as more tears raced down my cheeks. I was completely, utterly shocked that she, a medical doctor, could be so unemotional about such a big part of my life. She didn't even make an apology for this.

Well-meaning friends often tell me that "God knows what is best" and "Please, Heather, try to focus on the good things in your life." Still, my empty heart keeps screaming, "Yeah, right. What kind of blessings are there in losing a baby? It's not like I have been blessed with another one!"

People assure me that "it will happen." How can they be so certain? What if God chooses to never allow us to get pregnant? I wrote in my journal:

I'm angry! I'm sad! I'm frustrated. I just want to get pregnant so badly, and I can't. I hate waiting for my period to come every single month. I feel like nobody knows what I am going through. I know that there are women out there who try for many years to get pregnant, and even spend a lot of money to do so, and still they are unable to conceive. But I still feel alone in my pain. There is a hole in my heart. I can feel it. It is March 6 and it has been almost eight months since I delivered Isabella. The inevitable has happened again. My period has arrived, and I am succumbed with sadness. My patience is waning. I feel defeated. Does God even want me to get up off my bathroom floor? The Bible says that with everything, by prayer and supplication, we should present our requests to God. Why do I feel like I have asked and asked, and yet am continually denied? I'm about ready to stop asking, and just forget about trying to get pregnant. I wish I could just stop caring.

Still, God has been teaching me about closure. I do not think that closure means boxing up all the things that remind me of Isabella. I think that it is easier for me to move on by remembering her, and her impact on my life. I have a small piece of furniture that I have adorned with special reminders of Isabella. I keep a framed ultrasound picture, some Bible verses that have given me encouragement, the little man and rock statue, and a candle that Sally and Pattie gave to me to mark the first anniversary of the day Isabella should have been born.

I have realized that moving on with life doesn't mean that you no longer have sad, emotional days. I still get that empty ache in my belly and in my heart. I ache for another baby. But when those days come, I find it comforting to hold onto those things that make me feel closer to Isabella.

I am venturing into the next phase of my grieving process. I do not use the "closure" term. Rather, I like "embracing life." I want to enjoy living and to let my life experiences change me into the person that God wants me to be. I believe God will give me the strength to look forward to my future, instead of allowing me to wish for a future that I cannot have.

CHAPTER

Ten

LITTLE EARTHQUAKES

Before I even realized what it was or where it came from, there it was: An aftershock, a little reminder earthquake.

One day I was embracing life, excited about the future. Then I was hit with a memory of Isabella. With little warning, tears streamed down my face, confusion flooded my mind, and I began to question life, and God's hand in my life. Why? Why? Why did this have to happen to me?!? Why can't God just bless me with a child? Why do I have to feel sad all the time? Then, I began to wonder, why am I feeling this way? Why now? I was doing great just a minute ago. Now I feel like I should just go curl up in my bed.

My first aftershock came when I was taking a shower the weekend before Thanksgiving, the weekend prior to the one Isabella was supposed to be born. I had returned home from the gym, excited to find an aerobics class that I enjoyed open on Thanksgiving morning. What a great way to start the day! I was trying to make Thanksgiving Day an ordinary day. I did not want to get together with family, and I really did not want to celebrate the same way I might have, had Isabella lived. As I jumped into the shower, I began to think about what I would actually do on Thanksgiving Day. How would I fill my hours?

Adam would be working a 24-hour shift as a paramedic, and I knew I would have to be around people or I would likely get depressed. It might not be so bad spending the day with my family, but I knew that my sister's little girl, my niece Kayleigh, would remind me of my loss. As I thought about my family, how much we all love and adore

147

my niece, I became increasingly jealous, jealous that I could not share my baby with everyone, jealous that we would never get to watch my Isabella grow. Standing in the shower, I let the water get hot enough to burn my back. Sobs wracked my body. It was in this moment that I realized why it was hard for me to spend time with my niece, even though I was always happy to be in her presence.

I am jealous that my mom can show Kayleigh, every day if she wants to, how much she loves and cares for her. I feared that since Thanksgiving is a hard day for me anyway, it would only be worse if I had to watch my mom and Kayleigh together. Instead, I decided to spend the day with Adam at his firehouse.

Thanksgiving will always be a holiday of remembering Isabella. There are other anniversaries throughout the year as well that will make me cry for the life I had planned. As I write this, nearly a year has passed since I found out I was pregnant with Isabella. Adam and I will spend this day together, too. And still I wondered if God had not allowed us to get pregnant yet so that we were able to have this year of grief. Maybe He knew that we needed this year to remember Isabella's short life.

I still feel angry that my baby died. But I am also beginning to be grateful for the journey. I continue to hold on to the words in Jeremiah 29:11,

"For I know the plans I have for you, declares the Lord. Plans to prosper you and not to harm you. Plans to give you a hope and a future."

I love that God knows my heart's desire, but I also trust that He knows the perfect timing for us to have another child. Aftershocks. Our little reminder earthquakes.

CHAPTER
Eleven
MOTHER'S DAY AND EPT

May 7, 2004, two days before Mother's Day and I have reached the point of impatience. I must satisfy my curiosity. I must take that dreaded pregnancy test. The days prior to taking the test are calculated. They start something like this: On the fifth day before my period, I tell myself that I have not been keeping track of my cycle. I am not certain what day I will begin to ride the dreaded crimson tide. On the fourth day before my period, I continue trying to convince myself that I am not pregnant, and I do not know when my period will come. Throughout the day, I find excuses to look at the calendar.

On the third day before my period, I start counting out the days until my period's arrival. I am still trying to convince myself that I am not pregnant. On the second day before my period, I think about the early pregnancy test stored beneath my bathroom sink. Still, I tell myself it would be waste of money to use the test at this point.

The day before my period, I give in to the temptation. I rip open the EPT test box. I don't really need to read these instructions. They are burned into my brain. Still, I read them once again to reassure myself that I am doing everything correctly. (As though there is more than one way to pee on a stick). As I read the instructions for about the twentieth time, I begin to second guess myself, *"Should I take the test? It might be a waste of money if it's negative. But, if it's positive…Oh forget it, I have to take the test. I want to find out—NOW—whether or not I am pregnant."*

As I take the test, I remind my self. Self: *"This is no big deal.*

No big deal. Got that? I am merely taking the test so that I can know whether or not to expect my period."

Simultaneously, I dream about how exciting it will be to tell everyone I am pregnant...on Mother's Day!

When I finish the test, and wait the allotted minutes, I see that I am not pregnant. As the tears stream down my face, I silently remind myself that this was the answer that I was expecting. But it seems no matter the preparation, I am still heartbroken to know another month has gone by without a child.

Some of my friends told me that when they tried to get pregnant, it happened when they stopped trying and simply didn't think about it anymore. They say you have to be calm and to not stress out your body. Impossible! Maybe God has wired me differently. I have tried telling God that I do not want to worry myself about getting pregnant. I told Him it would happen with His timing, not mine or Adam's. Still, these thoughts only lasted until the next month, when my cycle was due to begin again, and when I pulled out another EPT test.

I know that God's timing is perfect. But I am a little anxious. I find excitement in holding onto the hope of what next month might bring.

CHAPTER
Twelve
CLOUD 9 OF HOPE

Today is June 16, 2004. Last year at this time, I was carrying Isabella, hoping and praying God would allow her to live. Now, one year later, I am still holding onto hope that God will bless me soon with a child. As of this moment I am not yet pregnant, but there is always a small glimmer of hope in the back part of my mind. Maybe, just maybe, this month is the month.

Some people believe that this kind of thinking, wishing, is foolish. But I believe there are two kinds of people in this world. Those who get excited about something right away, and those whose excitement is reserved, as they await a "sure thing." I have heard it said that people who hold their excitement in check do so because they fear there may be bad news ahead. They do not want to come crashing off of Cloud 9.

I myself am a Cloud 9-er kind of person. I cannot withhold my excitement. The moment I am one day late with my period I am already dreaming about the cutest way to tell my husband that we are pregnant. I can't help it. Fortunately, I have nearly perfected the inevitable crash landing that follows that kind of Cloud 9 news.

I suppose there is a positive side to being so easily excited. I am usually excited about good news for longer than I am depressed about bad news. Prior to the start of my period, I sometimes let myself get excited for days before my cycle starts. Once my period does start, I'm usually sad for a day or two, but then I go right back to focusing on getting pregnant the next month.

While this system may seem like a roller coaster ride of high and low emotions, especially for those not easily excitable, let me assure you that it works for me. For me, the initial excitement is always more fun than when you try to save it until it's a "for sure thing." If I had waited the traditional three months to be excited about my pregnancy with Isabella, I would have missed out. It was at three months pregnant that I learned something was wrong with her.

One thing I have learned: Nothing is a "for sure thing" on earth. The only thing I can hold onto is my hope in God. God has given me the gift of hope, yet at the same time He has taught me how to live beyond a deadline. It's been a tough year, but now I no longer have my agenda for when I would like to get pregnant.

It's up to God's agenda. I didn't get to this place overnight, but I'm still hopeful to reaching Cloud 9 again.

CHAPTER
Thirteen
BROWN GRASS, GREEN GRASS

I had every intention of ending my portion of the book with Chapter 12. But then, God answered my prayers. I wish I could tell you that I am now six months pregnant—or that I'd already given birth to a healthy child. But that was not God's plan.

I found out that I was pregnant again on June 17, 2004. I felt like I was on Cloud 9 and I never wanted to come down. Since it was the weekend before Father's Day, I decided to tell my husband our good news by buying him a Father's Day balloon. I remember Adam walking into the house. He looked at the balloon. Then he looked at me and said, "Really? We're going to have a baby?"

I started crying as I shrieked, "Yes!"

After about 20 minutes of screaming, hugging and crying, I told Adam that I wanted to go tell the world. The first person we set out to tell was his mom. When Sandy saw us from a distance, she just knew. We started screaming at the same time, and we were crying as we ran toward each other to embrace. We were so excited that we fell to the ground, laughing, crying and screaming with joy. As soon as we calmed ourselves, we stopped and thanked God for the blessing He gave to us.

Unfortunately, Adam had plans for the rest of the day, but I told him that I could not keep this news to myself. After all, I had been waiting and praying for this day. I ran around town telling everyone and anyone who would listen. I got a little annoyed when some of my friends (in a very kind and loving way, of course) tried to tell me not to get my hopes up too soon. While I appreciated their care for me, I believed in my heart that God would not be so cruel as to take away another baby.

About eight weeks into my pregnancy, I began spotting. July 9 was already a sad day for me. It was the day, just one year prior, that I had found out that Isabella had died. I called the advice nurse right away, and she told me not to worry because spotting is common in a pregnancy. But, of course, I worried.

I called Adam and began to cry as I told him what was happening. He, too, told me not to worry, and tried to calm me. The spotting stopped, only to return that Sunday. Adam and I were on our way out to lunch, trying to do something special for July 11, the day that I had delivered Isabella. I called my mother-in-law, Sandy, in a panic and sobbed as I explained the situation. I could tell, even from over the phone lines, she also wanted to cry. Sandy made several phone calls, looking for women who had spotted during their pregnancies, and actually found several. This was encouraging news to me, and I began to think that maybe this was just a little bump in the road. Over the next couple of weeks, I spotted off and on, but tried not to worry too much.

Two weeks later: We went to the hospital because I started bleeding. I called Sandy, frightened that something might be wrong with my baby, but also still believing that nothing could possibly be wrong with this baby, since God had already taken one baby from me. Sandy reassured me that nothing was wrong, and read us some Bible scripture from a passage in Joel. The passage speaks of Joel going through some difficult times in his life, but then God promises Joel that He will bless him, that his pastures will turn from brown to green. Our take on this reading was that once the pastures turn green they would not turn back to brown again.

This passage encouraged me since we had gone through such difficult times with Isabella, and then tried to get pregnant. Since God had blessed us with a pregnancy, we believed that God would not turn our green grass back to brown.

When we arrived at the hospital, the nurse who checked me in made me feel stupid for even being at the hospital, causing me to question why we were there, since spotting during the first three months of a pregnancy is considered normal. Sandy kept reminding me, however, that because we pay for health insurance, we were well within our rights to use it whenever it was needed.

As I walked into the examination room, Adam asked me if I wanted his mom to come with us. I said no, because I did not think that anything was really wrong. After all, I was only there to get peace of mind. Once the doctor began the ultrasound, he immediately determined that we were only eight weeks along (we thought we were at least 10 weeks along). As he continued the ultrasound, the screen was turned away from me, and he spent several minutes, I believe, looking for a heartbeat. As I lay there on the bed, I remember trying to reassure myself, whispering, "the grass is turning green, the grass is turning green."

Finally, the doctor turned the screen to us, and showed us that there was no heartbeat. No heart beat.

"No! No! No!" I began screaming. "This can't be happening again! I can't go through this again!"

When Sandy walked into the room, she was sobbing. Through racked sobs of my own, I said, "The grass is not turning green yet."

As I look back on this sad day, I am still unable to make sense of it. I don't know why we had a second baby taken from us. It's just not fair. I often wonder what God was doing the day I found out I was pregnant again. Was He rejoicing with me, or was He crying because He knew what was to come?

I lost my second baby at the end of July, and as I write this, it is the middle of October. I am not pregnant yet, and I wish I could say that I am wholeheartedly excited to get pregnant again. I am afraid of that day actually. I am scared that God will take another baby from me. I am scared that I will not be able to get excited, because I have had my heart broken. I hate the thought of not getting excited the day I find out that I am with child.

And I miss my Isabella. One weekend I was on a retreat with many of the women from the church I attend. During the Sunday morning segment of our worship time, a woman from the church, and a dear friend of mine, Eileen, got up and told her story. She told of how her mom, too young and unprepared for a child, had tried to have an abortion. The abortion did not turn out as planned though, because Eileen survived and was given up for adoption. Her story included pictures of her tiny little body the day she was born, arriving 12 weeks early, and weighing only two and a half pounds. Seeing these pictures of such a small infant reminded me of Isabella, and I just began sobbing.

I told God how much I missed Isabella. It was in that moment that God gave me a special gift. I felt like I was having a conversation with Isabella. I felt like she was saying, "Hi, Mommy."

When I told her again how much I missed her and loved her, she said, "I know, and I love you too, but don't worry about me, because I am with Jesus." Then, with tears streaming down my cheeks, I felt Jesus wrap his arms around me, hold me tight, and once again remind me, saying, "Don't worry, I have amazing things planned for you. Just hold on a little big longer."

And that's what I am doing. Holding on tight, and waiting for that green grass.

Epilogue April 2007

I am a now a mother of two. Let me back up though, and tell you how I got to this point.

After a third miscarriage, we were referred to the infertility department. I was now considered infertile. After doing numerous tests, the doctors concluded that there was no medical explanation for why I was unable to carry a baby to full term. They encouraged us to consider invitro fertilization or adoption.

Adam said that he would support whatever decision I made. Many people had asked me during the years of miscarriages if I had considered adoption. It wasn't until March of 2006 though that I felt like God had given me a peace about adopting. When I told Adam that I was ready to adopt, he was very excited. He said that he felt like this is what God wanted us to do, and was hoping that I would come to the same conclusion.

That very night I got on the computer and began researching adoption. It all seemed so overwhelming. Thankfully, we got connected with an amazing organization, called *Lifetime Adoption*. We filled out their application, and were in contact with them immediately. Once the process began, everything happened so fast. By the end of March we submitted 50 profiles including pictures of us, our home, and our family. Then, Lifetime immediately sent them out to prospective birth moms.

The following week we got a call from Lifetime saying that they had a birth mom who liked our profile, and wanted to talk to us on the phone. That night Adam and I both talked to her, and immediately there was a connection.

By the end of the week, we had met her, and were considered matched to being able to adopt her baby. Less than four months later, we were in the delivery room watching our baby, London, being born. It has been one year since we first met London's birth mom. London is now eight months old, and is the biggest blessing. Since adopting London, God has doubly blessed us. London is going to be a "big" sister. We found out six weeks after London was born, that I was pregnant. I am now the proud mom of Geneva Grace who was born May 19, 2007. I am having so much fun being a mom to my two daughters.

Through all of this, the biggest lesson that I have learned, is that God is looking at the bigger picture. We only have a very small window of information, but God is able to see what we do not yet even know. Every time I lost a baby, He knew that there was a child out there who would be a perfect fit into our family. He knew that she would need us as much as we needed her. In the midst of trials I have learned that the only thing that we can do is to trust in the passage Jeremiah 29:11, and trust that God wants the best for our lives.

Acknowledgements

I am especially grateful to my husband, Adam, for being my stronghold. Somehow, you were able to be sensitive to my grief, and yet remain strong for me. Our marriage was made stronger because of our daughter, Isabella.

To my sister Jennifer and my grandmother, Joyce Houser, who acted on my mother's behalf during my labor and delivery. Jen, thank you for letting me "steal Kayleigh" at any given time. Grandma, thank you for letting me talk and cry with you.

To my mom and dad, Steve and Julie Hammond. How do I say thanks to the ones who taught me how to be a mom? You raised me to be a woman of integrity, which helped me through the darkest days of my life. I love you both.

To Jim and Sandy, thank you for loving and supporting me like I was your own daughter. I love you both.

To my brothers, Ryan, Justin, and Steven, thank you for coming to see Isabella. I know it was not easy, but I am proud of you and your visit meant the world to me.

To Aunt Sherri, for giving me the best gift I could ever have received. Isabella's blanket has been my most sacred treasure. You've lightened my grief since she was born.

To Aunt Janelle, thank you for your love and support, as well as sharing your story with me. Only God knows why these things happen; I think one reason is so that we can pass along our stories and words of wisdom to others. Your honesty inspires and strengthens me.

I thank all my extended family, for your prayers, love and support.

To Marge, thank you for caring for me and Adam.

To Helen and Arvil, you both are such a huge part of our lives, and you have always known just when to call or stop by to see how we are doing. Thank you for all your prayers and support.

To Jennifer Woodmansee: God brought you into my life at just the right time, knowing that I would need friends like you during my journey.

To Sarah Garcia: Being a mom, you always seemed to know exactly what I was feeling. Thank you, too, for your early reading of my story. And to my girls, Jenna Morrow, Sarah Hale, Sarah Warwick, Danielle Londre, and Stephanie Palmer, thank you for being my friends and for letting me share Isabella with you.

To all the staff, parents and children at Kiddie Kampus Preschool in Los Gatos, California, for your love, your kindnesses and understanding.

And finally, to Pattie Zylka and Sally Spencer: I believe that you both are a huge reason that my grieving process has gone as well as it has. Meeting together was like therapy for me. I love you both.

With Love,

Heather

San Jose, California
December 20, 2005

Many Thanks

Thank you, Dear Reader, for taking the time to let us share our stories with you. Our hope and prayer is that when *you* are faced with *losing normal*, you will rely on the God of peace and comfort to see you through.

To our prayer partners, Ann Addington, Helen Maples, Julie Hammond, and Sandy Cheney, who have bathed this project in prayer. For your love, support, and faithfulness we say thank you, thank you, thank you!

And to our very first editor, Kim Karloff, PhD, who became our friend as well as our mentor. You provided us with a safe haven where we could share our stories and our hearts. Thank you for your talent, and your uncanny ability to "hear" our voices.

With our love,

Sally, Pattie, & Heather

Los Gatos, California
March 9, 2006

THE RIGHTEOUS
CRY OUT, AND
the Lord hears them;
HE DELIVERS THEM FROM
ALL THEIR TROUBLES.
The Lord is close
TO THE BROKENHEARTED AND
SAVES THOSE WHO ARE
CRUSHED IN SPIRIT.

PSALM 34:17&18